Montague Davenport

Under the gridiron

a summer in the United States and the far West, including a run through Canada

ISBN/EAN: 9783744744645

Printed in Europe, USA, Canada, Australia, Japan

Cover: Foto ©ninafisch / pixelio.de

More available books at **www.hansebooks.com**

Montague Davenport

Under the gridiron

a summer in the United States and the far West, including a run through Canada

UNDER THE GRIDIRON

A SUMMER IN THE UNITED STATES AND THE FAR WEST,

INCLUDING

A RUN THROUGH CANADA.

BY

M⸱ DAVENPORT.

ILLUSTRATED.

London:
TINSLEY BROTHERS, 8, CATHERINE STREET, STRAND

1876.

INTRODUCTION.

IT has been frequently remarked, that everyone who has been away from his native land on a journey of any kind beyond that of an ordinary excursion or pleasure trip, considers it his duty to inflict upon the public a book on the subject, although the story may be one oft told before.

In the present instance, although there doubtless are many existing works upon America, comprising the history of its States and Cities, with their various populations, and other statistical information, I am not aware of any of the present nature; and am inclined to believe that the experiences of a summer tour through the States and Canada may prove of some little use, and probably not altogether devoid of interest, to those who on pleasure bent propose visiting the New World. I purpose, then, to give an outline, taken from my diary, of a tour during the summer months of 1875, extending over a distance of more than fifteen thousand miles.

To this I have added a Table of Distances (p. 140), between New York and fifty or sixty of the principal cities, which will prove an assistance to the tourist in his calculations as to the disposal of his time.

In explanation of the title of this book, I may inform my readers not cognisant of the fact, that in nautical slang, "The Gridiron," is only another name for the American ensign.

MONTAGUE DAVENPORT.

CONTENTS.

Chapter I.

OFF!
PAGE

Hints as to Luggage—Steam Lines—Liverpool—Outward Bound—Queenstown and the Mails 1

Chapter II.

SNEAKING THE POND.

Life on Shipboard—Fellow Passengers—Regulations—Effects of the Swell—America 6

Chapter III.

BOSTON.

Carriage Hire—The Park—Bunker's Hill—A Question with the Customs—Boston Belles—The Fall River Route to New York 11

Chapter IV.

NEW YORK CITY.

Broadway—The Business Quarter—Wall Street—Brooklyn—The Bay—The Gridiron—Central Park—The Great Reservoir—Street Transit—The Air Line—Advertisements—Hotel Life 18

Chapter V.

THE QUAKER CITY.

PAGE

Philadelphia—Sambo—Chestnut Street, and more Marble —Fairmount Park and the Exhibition—Laurel Hill— Schuylkill and Delaware Rivers—Races at Point Breeze Park 27

Chapter VI.

BALTIMORE.

A Hundred Miles South—Driven from the Wharf—A Climb in the Dark—Beautiful Women—Unwelcome Visitors 32

Chapter VII.

WASHINGTON.

General Aspect—The Capitol—The White House—The Treasury—Dollars by the Million—General Lee's— Down the Potomac—Tomb of Washington 35

Chapter VIII.

VIRGINIA AND THE WHITE SULPHUR SPRINGS.

Near Gordonsville—Quiet Farming—A Corn Shuck Mattress—Real Thunderstorms—Insects and Birds— Coloured Labour—The Alleghany Mountains—Life at the Springs 40

Chapter IX.

OIIIO RIVER AND CINCINNATI TO ST. LOUIS.

PAGE

West Virginia—Kanawha River—Night on the Ohio—Negro Melodies—Porkopolis—Indiana and Illinois—Heat and Dust—The Great Steel Bridge 47

Chapter X.

THE QUEEN OF THE MISSISSIPPI.

St. Louis—Suggested Seat of the Government—Lafayette Park—Base Ball—Sunday in St. Louis—The Six Shooter 51

Chapter XI.

MISSOURI, KANSAS AND COLORADO.

Grasshoppers—Kansas City—The Plains—Sharp Eating—The Trapper and the Indians—The Boundless Prairie—Buffaloes—Prairie Dogs and Jackass Rabbits ... 54

Chapter XII.

DENVER AND THE ROCKY MOUNTAINS.

Denver—Long's and Pike's Peaks—A Wonderful Mountain Chain—Up Among the Rockies—Black Hawk—Central City—Novel Gambling—Idaho Springs—A Burning Forest—Gold Diggers—A Slice of Luck—Mountain Scenery—Torture on Wheels—Another Fire 59

Chapter XIII.

WYOMING, UTAH, AND SALT LAKE CITY.

The Highest Railway Station in the World—Wahsatch Mountains—Echo and Weber Canons—Ogden—A Smash Up—Great Salt Lake—The Mormon City—The Prophet and the Government—A Travelling Circus 68

Chapter XIV.

THE SIERRA NEVADAS.

The Great Deserts—Indians and their Squaws—California—Snow Sheds—Cape Horn—Marvellous Scenery—Harvest Time—Sacramento—San Francisco Bay ... 74

Chapter XV.

THE CITY OF THE GOLDEN GATE.

San Francisco—Hotels—Climate—The People—Sunday—A Street Preacher—Sea Lions—The Pacific Ocean—The Golden Gate—Woodward's Gardens—John Chinaman 79

Chapter XVI.

YO-SEMITE.

Snelling—Dudley's—Californian Driving—Practical Joking by the Indians—The Big Trees—The Valley—Rocks and Waterfalls—A Scorcher 85

Chapter XVII.

OMAHA, CHICAGO, AND DETROIT.

Silver Palace and Pullman Cars—Nebraska—Omaha—Julius Meyer—A Heavy Move—The New Chicago—Lake Michigan—Trade—Detroit—The River by Moonlight 91

Chapter XVIII.

NIAGARA.

The New Suspension Bridge — American Fall — Goat Island and the Rapids—The Horse Shoe—Whirlpool Rapids—The Great Whirlpool—Gone Over—The Burning Spring—Battlefields and Monuments... ... 97

Chapter XIX.

TORONTO, RIVER ST. LAWRENCE, AND MONTREAL.

A Long Street—The City—Lake Ontario—Kingston and Prescott—St. Lawrence River—The Thousand Islands Shooting the Rapids—Victoria Bridge—Montreal—A Great Church—L'Ile St. Hélène—Overladen 103

Chapter XX.

QUEBEC.

General Appearance—A Forsaken Citadel—The Fort—Heights of Abraham—Falls of Montmorency—An Indian Village—Up the St. Lawrence—Jigs and Reels 108

CONTENTS.

Chapter XXI.

LAKES CHAMPLAIN AND GEORGE.

PAGE

Last of Canada—Lake Champlain—Adirondack and Green Mountains—Lake George—The Islands—A Salute—Fort William Henry Hotel—A Drive to Glenn's Falls 113

Chapter XXII.

SARATOGA.

Monster Hotels—The Grand Union—Society—Life in the Streets—The Springs—The Race Course—Lake Saratoga—Glen Mitchell—A Garden Party—Youthful America—Dress and Diamonds... 117

Chapter XXIII.

THE MIGHTY HUDSON.

Albany and its Trade—Hudson River Steamers—The Catskill Mountains—Rip Van Winkle—Fishkill Mountains —River Scenery—West Point—Sing Sing—The Palisades—New York Bay 125

Chapter XXIV.

HOMEWARD BOUND.

Money Changing—Farewell—Sandy Hook—Saloon List —Globe Trotters—Porpoises—Ocean Spray—Signalling—Ireland—Our Cousins—Liverpool—Home Again 130

CONTENTS. xi.

Chapter XXV.

THE AMERICAN PEOPLE.

PAGE

Energy—Levelling—Representation—Brag—Storekeepers —General Character 135

Tables of Distances, &c. 140

LIST OF ILLUSTRATIONS.

	PAGE
ACROSS THE PRAIRIE	Frontispiece
ECHO CAÑON, UTAH	70
CROSSING THE SIERRA NEVADAS, CAPE HORN	76
SENTINEL ROCK, YO-SEMITE VALLEY	88
NIAGARA FALLS	98
THE THOUSAND ISLANDS	103
LACHINE RAPIDS, ST. LAWRENCE RIVER	105
HUDSON RIVER	127

CHAPTER I.

OFF.

HINTS AS TO LUGGAGE—STEAM LINES—LIVERPOOL—
OUTWARD BOUND—QUEENSTOWN AND THE MAILS.

THE facilities for travel are now so ample, and the American railway system so complete, that, given the necessary time, there are no places more easy of access than Canada, the States, and the Far West.

It may be as well to give a few hints to intending tourists, who have not been over the ground before. In the first place, with regard to luggage, take as little as you can conveniently manage with. The general mistake is, the idea that a great variety of costume is necessary, whereas the repeated packing and unpacking is often a source of great annoyance. What would suffice for a month's tour in Switzerland will quite answer the purpose,—say a small trunk and a travelling-bag of moderate dimensions. The trunk can be sent on to any principal town by the American system of registering, which is truly perfect, while the traveller may take three or four days to reach the same place, stopping, or, as Jonathan terms it, "lying over" at different points of interest *en route;* the bag carrying all pressing necessities. In our own case we took nearly double what we required, many articles never being used; hence the foregoing remarks.

The Steam Lines to America are so numerous that it must be left to the tourist to bestow his patronage wherever his inclination may lead him. The Cunard, Inman, White Star, National Companies, &c., all possess some of the most magnificent ships afloat, and replete with every comfort and convenience. The rates of passage vary very little, being about seventeen to twenty guineas, saloon, or thirty guineas return, extending over six months. My friend and I booked our berths in London by the Cunard Line, about a month beforehand, thus securing one of the best state-rooms—a matter worthy of consideration, as it is to be our home for ten or eleven days.

We will imagine the trunks to be packed, the leave-taking at Euston over, the last good wishes spoken, the handkerchiefs withdrawn from the carriage window, and the Liverpool express whisking us along at a speed of from forty to fifty miles an hour, bringing us after a run of five hours to the Lime Street Station of the London and North Western Railway. Having a day or two to while away before sailing, we visit friends in this great and busy city, and ride out by the coaches to Garston, Wavertree and Woolton.

It is the commencement of May, and the avenues of trees overhanging the Garston Road are bright with the fresh green of the bursting buds, while on our right, between the handsome villas of the Liverpudlians, we now and again catch a glimpse of the Mersey, some distance below us. That river offers attractions in the form of short steamboat excursions, and we run over to New Brighton and Rock Ferry.

From the river can also be viewed the magnificent docks, extending some three miles in length, which are the admiration of the world. Of the Public Buildings, St. George's Hall, with its renowned organ, statues, &c., must not be overlooked, and Brown's Library hard by deserves a visit.

With respect to Hotels, it would be invidious to draw any distinction where so many are excellent. We stay at the Washington, a great American house, and receive every satisfaction at moderate charges. The London and North Western Hotel is a handsome edifice, and has its patrons, as also the Adelphi, another favourite.

Having called at the Cunard Office, in Water Street, and received our instructions, we go on board the tender, at Prince's Landing Stage, and head up stream for about a mile, where the Cunarder, with her black funnel capped with red, is lying at her moorings. All is hurry and excitement; the last packages being hauled on board and lowered into the hold; the passengers rushing after their baggage to see it secure in their state rooms; the experienced travellers and old hands being more intent on securing the preferred seats at the table, which, once allotted, are retained for the voyage.

The first, second, and third bells have been rung; the tender is full of those departing for the shore, whilst the big ship, now free from her moorings, glides majestically away, a bright sun shining overhead, and a strong breeze blowing, which increases as we leave the Rock Fort Lighthouse behind, and get fairly into the Irish Sea.

Standing, looking over the quarter of this noble vessel, our veins swell with a sense of superiority as we meet the Manx Steamer at the mouth of the river; this ungenerous feeling is, I think, universally experienced when passing vessels bound on a pettier errand. The tourists on an Antwerp or Rotterdam steamer look down with a species of compassion on the excursion boat from Ramsgate, while that vessel's passengers, in their turn, regard the Woolwich Boat with absolute pity.

With a head-wind and sea we go romping down the Irish Channel, through the sulky-looking swells, smashing them disdainfully in two in a way it is a treat to witness.

It takes some little time to settle down into our places on board, and look around us, when we find that we number forty-one cabin passengers, with three hundred emigrants in the steerage, and learn that we are to embark as many more at Queenstown. The remainder of the day passes in a desultory manner, and we rise next morning to find ourselves running along the Irish Coast, and have to wait four hours in Queenstown Harbour for the mails. In the meantime, we take on board upwards of three hundred more emigrants, mostly Irish, and as boats surround the ship, chartered by Irish women who throw oranges up to the passengers, the money being returned by the same process, much amusement is caused by the Irish chaff and sundry mishaps that occur.

The mails at last safe on board, we are soon out of the Cove of Cork, bound for Boston, and, with our ship's nose to the westward, the Irish Coast soon fades from our view, our last sign of its whereabouts being the gleam from the Fastnet Light, at which we give a parting glance before turning in for the night.

CHAPTER II.

SNEAKING THE POND.

LIFE ON SHIPBOARD—FELLOW-PASSENGERS—REGULATIONS—EFFECTS OF THE SWELL—AMERICA.

LIFE on an American liner is so utterly the reverse of that on shore, yet at the same time so thoroughly enjoyable, if entered into with a will, that I must give a short description of how that time is passed.

Our first impulse on receiving from the Purser the printed list of the saloon passengers, is to endeavour, by each other's assistance, to identify them and form some idea as to the prospect of the voyage being passed in pleasant company or otherwise. The first day or two resemble the early dances at an evening party, but gradually our national reserve is melted and genial intercourse prevails.

We find our passenger list comprises a motley group. A quiet reflective Bostonian, with two ladies, who are returning after a twelvemonths' tour through Europe; a noted American poet; a retired line captain, going out to try his luck at anything that may turn up, who states his readiness to embark in any promising concern, from a sandwich shop upward; he is the life and soul of the ship—the jolliest among the jolly—in fact, a perfect Mark Tapley; a young gentleman with capital, weary of a lawyer's office, bound to Colorado, to essay farming with a friend already established there; a newly-married couple, off to British Columbia, to open up a lumber trade; a West-end clubsman, with a wondrous collection of fishing implements, to test the Canadian rivers and waters: he is an enthusiast in the art, and tells of much fishing in Scotland and Ireland, but the national love of change lures him from his accustomed haunts; an American Bank manager and family, returning from a visit to the old country, and apparently much impressed with the way business is conducted in the British House of Commons, having been a listener to several of the debates, and also much struck with our horses and equipages at the West-end and Parks; a satirical, but amusing, Scotchman, travelling in the dry goods line, and crossing for the fifty-fifth time, will suffice for examples. A sprinkling of ladies, who, however, with one or two exceptions, do not often come forward, owing to certain susceptibilities, of which more anon, complete the list.

Order and punctuality are the very soul of the ship, the following being the rules observed by all, and unalterable : Breakfast at half-past eight. Luncheon at twelve. Dinner at four. Tea at half-past seven. Supper (ordered only by those still open to refreshment) nine till ten. Saloon lights put out at eleven. Stateroom lights at twelve. A liberal table is provided, and the passenger has only Father Neptune to thank if he do not appreciate it.

Provided also with a library, they can lose themselves among the popular works of the day who prefer such a course to the amusements on deck, which consist of shovel-board and quoits. The sweepstakes on the last figure of the day's run will enlist some subscribers, the day being determined from observations taken at noon, which hour arrives about thirty minutes sooner every day, going west, New York time being five hours earlier than London. After sunset there are whist, chess, draughts, backgammon, &c., which may be played in the saloon or smoking room on deck.

After leaving Queenstown, we soon begin to experience the long swell of the Atlantic, the vessel apparently dropping bodily. This persuasive movement of the ship causes many to appear as if deep in thought, and who, alas! when more advanced in their calculations, will join the ranks of those who are already actively engaged in casting up the difference between feeling sick and being sick. However, "Everything comes to him who waits," we are told, and except, in very rare instances, these distressing exercises come to an end, and a happy disregard of the ship's capers succeeds.

The bright days and moonlit nights pass by more quickly than anticipated, if one can find enjoyment and take an interest in the various scenes on shipboard; the spreading and taking in of sail, the heaving of the log, sighting and speaking other vessels, eastward and westward bound, the shoals of porpoises gambolling on the surface of the water, the cloud of gulls following the ship for any scraps thrown from the galley, the gorgeous sunsets, heavy rain storms shortly after blown away to leeward like a wall, and the constantly changing colour of the sea, all uniting to please the eye and fancy, while the keen and clear air gives a life and vitality to the feelings truly invigorating.

Nearing the banks of Newfoundland, we find the temperature many degrees colder, and sight an iceberg to the northward. We also experience two or three of the fogs peculiar to this region, and attributed to the influence of the Gulf Stream (and for what has that said stream not been held accountable?); we also see some whales spouting, and early one morning, when the fog accommodatingly clears off, find ourselves within sight of the American Coast, and in smooth water, with a brilliant sun overhead, steaming up among the Islands and Forts of Boston Bay; and, as we near the wharf, meet another of our Line just out of dock, homeward bound, and give each other a passing cheer.

CHAPTER III.

BOSTON.

CARRIAGE HIRE—THE PARK—BUNKER'S HILL—A QUESTION WITH THE CUSTOMS—BOSTON BELLES —THE FALL RIVER ROUTE TO NEW YORK.

PILED up on the slope of the hills, with the great gilt dome of the Capitol or State House surmounting all, this city, viewed from the sea, presents an imposing appearance. At first sight it appears almost surrounded by water, so winding is the harbour and numerous are the bridges connecting the different parts of the town.

We take leave of our fellow-passengers, pass our baggage through the Customs—a matter of no very great difficulty—and drive off to the "Tremont" Hotel, Tremont Street, the name arising from the City standing upon three hills, and having been called the Tri-montane City.

By the way, it may be as well to hint that when taking a carriage it is desirable and more profitable that a bargain be struck before hiring, this city and New York being unrivalled in their charges—high when compared with those of Europe. For instance, for the journey from the wharf to the hotel, about a mile and a half, two of us, with two trunks, the charge was three dollars and a half, about thirteen shillings.

A word also about American hotels. A fixed charge, varying from three to five dollars per day, is made, which includes everything, a separate bedroom to each person amongst other things. Meals are on the table at certain times for about two hours each, there being in fact always one or the other on hand.

Tremont, Washington, and State Streets are the principal in this city, and possess fine shops (here termed stores), apparently driving a busy trade.

In the very midst of the city stands the Common, a park extending over fifty acres, and beautifully wooded, adjoining the Public Garden, with its ornamental water. This noble greensward, with its forest trees, offers an agreeable shade from the sun, which is now powerful, and makes us feel that we have plunged all at once into summer. The trees contain numerous little cots fixed among the branches, for the shelter and breeding of small birds, which are much admired and well cared for; this is noticeable in most of the large cities.

In the evening, after sundown, this spot presents a most attractive spectacle. The innumerable little white boats and water velocipedes on the lake, flitting hither and thither, each bearing a lantern, added to the myriads of lamps to be seen glistening through the trees give a character to the scene of almost fairy-like beauty.

On the west side of the Park, facing an equestrian statue of Washington, is Commonwealth Avenue, a long line of really handsome residences. At the south side is Tremont Street, where do congregate tram-cars innumerable, while on the north side is Beacon Street, with the State House rearing its head above all.

Among the numerous churches, the Immaculate Conception Roman Catholic Cathedral is well worth visiting, and the fine spire of one in Park Street is worthy of notice. A list of the others can be seen in the local guide book, to be which this does not pretend.

A ride out of about five miles by the tram-car to Forest Hills gives a good sample of the country round. The cars are in many cases open, and better than ours; the rails worse. Another short ride in the opposite direction brings us to Bunker's Hill, where an immense granite obelisk commemorates the Irish rise the Yanks took out of the Britishers in days gone by. From here can be seen Harvard University, some little distance away, and hard by is a handsome memorial to the men of Charleston, who fell in the '61 war for the Union.

Wines and spirits are to be obtained here only at fabulous prices, with the natural consequence that little wine is seen at the dinner table, even at the best hotels. Iced water is swallowed by the pailful at every available opportunity, as also iced milk, a favourite drink at all meals.

A profusion of oysters is here, and, free from the pecuniary fine imposed at the present time on their consumption at home, we pay our respects to them from time to time. Lobsters and other shell fish are also very plentiful and cheap.

I may here mention an incident connected with Boston to show how advisable it is that any packages but personal luggage be sent through a shipping agent. We brought over a small set of communion plate, value about £5, a present from a friend to one of the Bishops, and were informed, on stating the contents of the parcel to the Custom House officer, that a duty of twelve dollars was payable, nearly half the value, but as we declined to pay, were to argue the case out the following day, as there appeared some doubt on the subject. Accordingly in the morning, after interviewing two officials and ascending in a factory lift, we were taken across to the Custom House, where some more twisting and turning occurred. In the end, these sapient officers found out that communion plate was exempt from duty. A paper marked " Free," with two signatures attached, was then handed to us, with instructions to present it at the wharf, where we should receive the box without further trouble. To the wharf, a mile and a half distant, we walked in a blazing sun, having also to cross the water by the ferry, only to learn that the wretched box had been sent up to the very place we had come from. Having retraced our steps, and waited some twenty minutes, the box was brought, with a demand for half a dollar for truckage. This fairly raised our ire, and on our reminding them that it had been illegally detained, and that we ought to be compensated for our trouble, it was allowed to go free. I mention this, as many going out are requested by friends to take sundry packages, often causing great inconvenience, and which can be sent in the regular way without any trouble and at a moderate charge.

The Boston belles dress well, and in the extreme of fashion, their clothing fitting them as tightly as skins. Being the first of the sex I have seen in America, I take especial notice, and find that as a rule they are slight in build, but with elegant figures. Some of these figures, however, so charming in outline, are, I imagine, mainly attributable to the exertions of the *modiste*, as displayed openly in the shops are certain different articles which are described as "furniture for ladies," who have to be fixed and fitted up before entering their dresses—in short, the wearer made to fit the dress. Many of the little girls wear costumes of white cashmere, with boots of same material, and are somewhat French in their appearance.

Horses are good but small, and the traps wonderfully light, after the style of the sulkies used in trotting matches, with harness of a similar character. How they stand the stony streets is a marvel.

Bidding adieu to the beautiful city of Boston, we travel by the Old Colony Railroad, running through some pretty country to Fall River, a distance of forty-nine miles, and embark on the steamship "Providence," for New York, *via* Long Island Sound.

To describe this vessel in detail would take more space than I am inclined to allow. She is a huge specimen of the American river steamer. Three hundred and seventy-three feet long, eighty-three fee beam, and three thousand tons register. She is driven by enormous side wheels, the sponson being carried right fore and aft. Built with five decks, the Grand Saloon is twenty-one feet in height, and illuminated by crystal gaseliers. The metal fittings are plated, and the furniture, grand piano, &c., of a costly description. A concert is held every evening, with a fine band; this boat, with her sister, "the Bristol," running at night to land their passengers in the morning. Below are dining and supper saloons, drinking bars, barber's shop, &c., whilst around are countless state rooms, their windows looking outward. The steward, under-stewards, and servants are all blacks, with smart uniforms.

The cost of these acmes of marine splendour was 1,250,000 dollars each, or a quarter of a million sterling. A dense fog the following morning delays us some three hours, the doleful and deep-noted fog horn sounding at intervals, other fog-bound steamers responding, dog fashion, until, at last, the fog lifts, when passing through Hell Gate, and by many factories and busy waterside industries, we reach New York at noon.

CHAPTER IV.

NEW YORK CITY.

BROADWAY—THE BUSINESS QUARTER—WALL STREET—
BROOKLYN—THE BAY—THE GRIDIRON—CENTRAL
PARK—THE GREAT RESERVOIR—STREET TRANSIT
—THE AIR LINE—ADVERTISEMENTS—
HOTEL LIFE.

ARRIVING here in a soaking rain, our first impressions, as we rattle through the slush and over the stones of the streets in a ponderous vehicle of last century pattern, are not favourable, and we gladly retreat into comfortable quarters at the St. Nicholas Hotel, Broadway, where, from the windows, we can watch the traffic passing, much after the character of Cheapside.

Not until evening does Jupiter Pluvius empty his watering pot, when we take a car to visit the Grand Opera House, built by Fisk, who was bored by a six-shooter and sent where Erie bonds are useless. Although a performance is advertised to take place, we find, to our chagrin, the theatre shut up. A knot of people is collected outside, and the only information we can obtain from a police officer, in reply to our query is: "I guess it's closed," and no more. We walk back down Broadway, and find our way into a smaller theatre, where we are amused by a piece entitled "The Frauds of New York," presenting, what I trust is, an exaggerated illustration of every species of villainy as practised in this city. By day we go down into the business quarter, and melt some of our letters of credit into bills and stamps, the latter term being applied to the fractional currency. Throughout the States (California excepted) we never meet with coin, except the five-cent piece, known as "a nickel," and the bronze cents and two-cent pieces, corresponding with our pence and half-pence.

The business men of New York do not offer sacrifice to Mrs. Grundy in the matter of attire—clerks and assistants in banks, offices, and shops sitting without coat or waistcoat enjoying their cigars, and endeavouring to keep cool in a way that would severely shock a London banker, and destroy the peace of mind of our prim solicitors.

Browsing round among the chief buildings, we pay visits to the Treasury and Customs, also the Cotton

Exchange, where a great and noisy sale is proceeding; then into the Stock Exchange, in Wall Street, where, from the visitors' gallery, we gaze upon the scene below. The noise and excitement is tremendous. Groups of men, some in linen coats and straw hats, others in billycocks and flannel shirts, are shouting and yelling vociferously, many appearing mad with ánger. The more than usually riotous proceedings are, we afterwards learn, attributable to the news of Eríes being thrown into liquidation.

The streets in this quarter are narrow, and the buildings crowded together. This must inevitably be the case. Every square foot of land is occupied, and there is no more; this portion of the city being surrounded on three sides by water, which can be seen at the end of nearly every street.

The ferries are numerous, and are, in fact, floating bridges, carrying horses, carriages, carts, &c., with hundreds of passengers. The system is excellent, and commands an immense traffic. Brooklyn, Jersey City, Hoboken, Staten Island, and other places can all be reached by this means, and these several little trips give the tourist a fair idea of the position of New York City.

The first named, lately of such unfortunate notoriety, is beautifully situate, having streets, churches, and stores quite equal to the great city. Here, the car can be taken to Greenwood Cemetery, well worth a visit, as, from the highest point, the Plateau, what may almost be called a bird's-eye view of New York can be obtained.

Lying like a map at our feet, the City of New York can be seen, with its numerous surroundings—New Jersey, Hoboken, Staten Island, and the Hudson River, with the Palisades—also the harbour, studded with vessels of every rig and nationality; the great white river steamers, rushing to and fro, being conspicuous objects in the picture; while entering, or leaving, may frequently be seen one of the great mail steamers, or a three-masted schooner—a favourite rig here—ploughing along under a cloud of canvas. Here can be seen the flags of all nations, predominant amongst all being the Stars and Stripes, or, as Jack terms it, "the Gridiron."

This cemetery is one of the largest in the world, and is laid out with great care and taste; its lakes and groves, with many fine examples of statuary and monumental designs, rendering it a scene of much interest and attraction.

A favourite drive from New York is to Prospect Park, near here, possessing a fine natural grove of trees. The ferry, however, has at present to be crossed, the new east river bridge not yet being completed. This said suspension bridge, the piers of which give a fair idea of what the rest of the structure will be when finished, will allow the tallest ship to sail beneath it, and is intended to be a masterpiece of its kind.

Central Park, about four miles from the City—the chief resort in the afternoon for all the fashionable world of New York—possesses great natural scenery in the way of rocks and trees, and is well preserved and kept up. There are some miles of walks, well shaded by trees, while the pink and white lilacs and Westeria in full bloom abound everywhere. A large and winding lake occupies a prominent place in the amusements, a service of boats being provided to row the visitor round at a moderate charge. There is also a Zoological Garden and some statuary.

The drive round and about comprises some eight miles of road, and carriages of every description, filled with richly-dressed ladies, may be seen here in hundreds, after the manner of our Row. Horse riding does not obtain in the States, and is rarely seen, the ambition of the thriving American being to drive a pair of fast trotters almost at racing speed; and some slashing trotters display on the principal drive, which is freely watered.

On the undulating greenswards may be seen hundreds of children, with their attendant nurses, black and white; while in one part is a steam whirligig, or merry-go-round, similar to those in the Champs Elysées at Paris.

At the top of the Park is seen the great reservoir, thirty-eight feet in depth, and covering a space of about a hundred and thirty acres. This enormous body of water is brought from a river forty-five miles distant, and supplies the whole of New York City.

The tram-cars are not equal to those at Boston, neither are the horses; the paving of roads and footways, with the exception of the Broadway, simply abominable, and much to be wondered at considering the surroundings. The cars run in all directions, at a charge of six to eight cents, and are used by everyone. There appears to be no limit to the number of passengers carried, the middle of the car and platforms at either end being filled with people, who will stand the whole journey sooner than wait five minutes for the following car.

Another curious mode of transit is the air line of railway. Some twelve feet above the ground, supported by a single row of pillars, and carried on cantilevers, a single line of a very narrow guage railway runs above the heads of the pedestrians on the pavement, and just on a level with the first floor windows. It is singular in its appearance, and certainly does not add to the beauty of the thoroughfare.

Architectural effect, however, is not allowed to

stand in the way of any supposed advantage to the business-man or shopkeeper, as witness the advertisements, which, even in the principal thoroughfares, cover the fronts of the houses, and the wire-gauze banners suspended across the streets, with notices of race meetings at Jerome Park, base ball matches, or stage plays to be performed. In short, advertising is carried to an extreme, which tends much to disfigure the appearance of the whole city.

Hotel life is of a kind the traveller cannot but admire. Palaces in their way, the hotels astonish the guest with the lavish display of white marble throughout. This is a distinguishing feature in most of the principal hotels throughout the States, and also in first-rate stores; the entrance halls, counters, chimney-glass frames, consoles, &c., being all of that material.

There are, as may naturally be expected in a great city, hotels of every description, and with varying scales of charges. The principal include Fifth Avenue, situated in the fashionable quarter, that street being the lounge of the upper ten, and where the latest fashions from Paris are always on view; the Gilsey House, St. Nicholas, Astor House, Grand Central, Metropolitan, &c., all of which are conveniently located.

The greater part of the ground floor is used as a hall, which, during the evening, is inconveniently crowded with outsiders as well as guests of the hotel, it being, as a rule, the public meeting place for men to conclude bargains in business, or speculate in the pools sold on any approaching races. The billiard saloons and smoking rooms are also filled with the public during this part of the day.

The style of living in any of these hotels is liberal in the extreme, every delicacy in season being supplied. Quoting from a *ménu* before me, the ordinary dinner at the St. Nicholas comprised, under the following heads, the number of dishes indicated:—Soups, two; fish, two; boiled, eight; roast, seven; cold, ten; *entrées*, ten; relishes, seven; vegetables, thirteen; pastry, eight; dessert, twelve; coffee. Total eighty. The above dishes include game and poultry, and the never-failing ice-creams.

Of theatres and concert-rooms there are some fifteen to twenty, of which the visitor to New York will learn all particulars at his hotel, programmes being always exhibited in the hall or reading-room; with racks filled with time tables, telling of sundry trips and excursions, far and near; while billiard saloons await him at every turn.

Although in a tobacco-growing country, we find cigars and tobacco dearer than at home, and our penny box of vesuvians fetches sevenpence.

There are many blacks here, or, as they prefer being

designated, " coloured people." In a side street we met a crowd of little niggers coming from school, and of all the funny little people we have seen, these little india-rubber juveniles, as they came along, laughing and jabbering, were the funniest.

Leaving New York, we carriage off to New Jersey City, crossing the Hudson river by the ferry, to the terminus of the Pennsylvania Railroad, whence we have a run of three hours through ninety miles of rather uninteresting country, crossing the Delaware river three or four times, and seeing many miles of it; also passing through Trenton, the capital of the State of New Jersey, with its iron foundries and works, to Philadelphia.

CHAPTER V.

THE QUAKER CITY.

PHILADELPHIA—SAMBO—CHESTNUT STREET AND MORE MARBLE—FAIRMOUNT PARK AND THE EXHIBITION—LAUREL HILL—SCHUYLKILL AND DELAWARE RIVERS—RACES AT POINT BREEZE PARK.

LYING on the Delaware river, a hundred miles from its mouth, Philadelphia, the capital of the State of Pennsylvania, covers more space than any city in the Union. Founded by William Penn, the Quaker, and the centre of his sect, it gained the above appellation.

We put up at the Continental Hotel, another mammoth. All the waiters here are black, the real Day and Martin and no compromise,—and very civil is Sambo as an hotel waiter. Black as ebony, he stands out in strong relief against the snow-white walls and marble columns, the contrast having an effect almost theatrical.

Situate in Chestnut Street, we see the pick of Philadelphian society, who affect this quarter, the stores in this street being, I should imagine, the finest in the world. Many of the shop fronts and entire houses are built of white marble, and must cost large sums, as the marble is brought from Italy. We notice several vessels in the Delaware river unloading the blocks.

The ground floors are of great height, and the interior fittings of the shops extravagant in their material, quite taking the sting out of those in London or New York. The streets all run at right angles, and with a sameness that almost amounts to severity. The tram-cars, as before, are the happy mediums employed to circulate the traveller to any point of the city, and also afford a shelter from the sun, who now puts forth his strength, and drives us out of the streets to seek the shady places in the suburbs.

Fairmount Park, just without the city, possesses great attractions. One of the largest public parks in existence, and on rising ground, it has great natural beauty, and commands a fine view over the river Schuylkill, which runs through it. In this park we see, in course of erection, the colossal building for the Centennial Exhibition of 1876. Adjoining, is Laurel Hill Cemetery, on the side of the hill of that name, from the summit of which extensive views can be obtained. The principal monuments to Philadelphia's noted citizens are of some interest.

Crossing the new bridge over the river, we take the boat up stream, and much enjoy the breeze, which we can now only taste on the water. The river is about twice the width of the Thames at Kingston, with thick foliage to the brink. The boats are small, and driven by a single paddle-wheel at the stern; they do not run a great distance up, but this part being cool and shaded, it is a favourite resort, especially on Sundays, and we more than once avail ourselves of it. At Fairmount, the starting place, is a very wide weir, picturesque in effect.

Another jaunt we take is by tram to the South Ferry, thence by steamer down the Delaware river. The water is well covered with vessels, mostly of the schooner class. On returning, we pass close to the wharves—coal, iron, and oil being the articles on which they grow fat here; also past the Navy Yard, where only two or three small war ships, and those of an obsolete pattern, are lying. Of course, the stars and bars are flying everywhere, and niggers about in hundreds.

A great race meeting also claims our attention, and we drive in the lightest of top buggies, with a pair, along roads six inches deep in dust, to Point Breeze Park, to assist at the last day's sport of the Grand

Spring Meeting. A charge of one dollar for entrance effectually keeps out the rabble, the whole ground being enclosed by high palings. The track is laid with sand, and is circular in form, the inside position being the one struggled for at the commeneement of the race. The card informs us that the purses of 500 dols. for the first, 450 for the second, and 150 for the third, are for trotting in harness, mile heats, best three in five.

Ten or eleven horses start for each heat, and the skilful driving to avoid collisions, excites our admiration. What with false starts, and remonstrances with threats of fines from the judge, they take some time to be run off, when we find the quickest heat has been run in 2 min. 27 sec. It appears a great pace in harness, but is frequently surpassed, and I believe I am correct in stating that the mile has been covered in 2 min. 14 sec. by that American trotting wonder, Goldsmith's Maid. Although somewhat sheltered from the sun's rays by the trees behind the Stand, we find the heat excessive, and the perspiring crowd hover round the drinking bar, seeking temporary relief in frequent draughts of iced Milwaukee beer, a kind of Lager.

We return by rail, and I may here mention, that as thirst prevails, there is provided in every railroad car and steamboat throughout the country small cisterns of iced water for the use of passengers, "free, gratis for nothing."

The detailed descriptions and histories of the public buildings, comprising Independence Hall, in Chestnut Street—famous for being the spot on which was signed the Declaration of Independence, July 4th, 1776 — universities, academies, hospitals, libraries, churches, Quakers' meeting houses, and theatres (amongst which last I may mention Walnut Street, where we see Boucicault in the "Shaughraun"), are they not written in the "Guide to Philadelphia and Environs"?

CHAPTER VI.

BALTIMORE.

A HUNDRED MILES SOUTH—DRIVEN FROM THE WHARF
—A CLIMB IN THE DARK—BEAUTIFUL WOMEN—
UNWELCOME VISITORS.

ENSCONCED in a comfortable saloon carriage of the Philadelphia, Wilmington, and Baltimore Railroad, and leaving Philadelphia behind, we speed away to the southward for nearly a hundred miles, through beautifully timbered and well watered country—passing Wilmington, the centre of a great peach-growing district, crossing the Susquehanna river, about two miles wide, where we have extensive views of Chesapeake Bay, and later on across Bush and Gunpowder rivers, the latter a mile in width; arriving, after a run of four hours, at Baltimore, chief town in the State of Maryland.

This is a seaport town of great commercial importance, and, like Boston, is built on rising ground, sloping down to the harbour, and is situate on the river Patapsco, connecting Chesapeake Bay. Near the wharves, and through the business quarter adjacent to the harbour, the streets are dirty, and a variety of odours assail us. The water appears to be almost stagnant, and, under the influence of a fierce sun, gives off exhalations more powerful than agreeable. In addition to this a stout hose is thrown in, and this same water dispersed by a pump in all directions over the roads near the quay, for the purpose of laying the dust. We are, in consequence, literally choked off the spot, and beat a hasty retreat. The chief trades here appear to be the putting up of oysters and lobsters in tins, and the manufacture of boots and shoes.

The higher and better portions of the town are noticeable for the numerous monuments which abound everywhere. The principal is a tall column, surmounted by a statue of Washington, pourtrayed in the act of resigning his commission. Impelled by the desire to see the view from the summit, I started for the ascent, my companion being less ambitious, and contented to sit quietly at the base. After walking about the town for some hours in a blazing sun, it proved an ordeal, for which the view around hardly compensated. The winding staircase is pitch dark, close and oppressive, and the visitor has to grope his way up three hundred and forty steps by the light of a hand lantern. On returning to earth, I was forced to admit that my fellow traveller had chosen wisely in taking it as climbed.

There are several other memorials, "The Battle" column in Fayette-street being conspicuous. The public buildings are numerous and of some merit, the dome of the Exchange being of noble proportions; also several churches, the Roman Catholic Cathedral being the finest.

Baltimore has more than her share of parks and cemeteries; and in the former may be seen of an afternoon the beautiful women for which this town is considered to bear away the palm. We do not find the hotel we put up at quite up to high water-mark, after New York and Philadelphia, as on retiring to our dormitories we discover the rooms thickly peopled with blackbeetles and cockroaches, who, by their calm effrontery, evidently believe that the war for the liberation of the blacks included them, while under the floors and behind the wainscot the rats are holding a well-attended revival meeting.

This is not altogether conducive to sound sleep, or what the lawyers term "quiet enjoyment;" consequently we do not feel much regret when, by the assistance of the Baltimore and Ohio railway, we put exactly forty-two miles between ourselves and this town, and are in the capital city of the United States.

CHAPTER VII.

WASHINGTON.

GENERAL ASPECT—THE CAPITOL—THE WHITE HOUSE—THE TREASURY—DOLLARS BY THE MILLION—GENERAL LEE'S—DOWN THE POTOMAC—TOMB OF WASHINGTON.

ON the Potomac river, in the district of Columbia, lies this magnificent city, called after the great American patriot, soldier, and statesman, whose name is attached to the principal streets, and whose statue is ever present throughout the chief cities of the republic.

We are located at the Arlington Hotel, nowhere surpassed in its excellent service, spacious saloons, and redundancy of comforts. To the proprietor, we are indebted for introductions to all the principal places of interest, whose name is legion. The general aspect of this city is of so distinct a character from any of the others, that although only an hour's journey from Baltimore, we can almost imagine ourselves in another world. Everything here is on a vast scale. The avenues one hundred and sixty feet wide, each street a hundred, none less; but little business is transacted, and it is a collection of parks, avenues, trees, statues, fountains, and palatial buildings, each beautiful in itself.

Its position is unrivalled, and I can quite believe its being the most lovely city on the globe. From whatever point we view it, we are struck by an air of refinement, repose, and overpowering grandeur unexperienced elsewhere.

Of all the great buildings in Washington, first and foremost in position and appearance is the Capitol, situated on the Capitol Hill, a most superb edifice, presenting a frontage of seven hundred and fifty feet by a depth of three hundred. It is built of granite and stone, and of colossal proportions. In it are comprehended the Senate and House of Congress, together with the Law Courts. Surmounting the whole is the dome, four hundred feet in height, which can be seen for many miles round, and for a great distance down the Potomac river. Beneath the dome are eight great paintings, recording the principal historical scenes in America's annals. There are also some fine statues of bygone presidents, among which is a striking one of the unfortunate Lincoln. The Senate and House of Congress are not remarkable for interior decoration, all being very plain. One cannot help noticing the great amount of space, fitted with seats, for the general public or audience, who can find ample accommodation to the tune of some thousands. There is also an extensive library, in addition to the many chambers allotted to officials. The cost of the whole was seventeen million dollars, nearly three and a half millions sterling, but which to erect at the present day would probably cost double that sum.

We also pay a visit to the White House, the official residence of the President, and are shown through all the private rooms. They are not remarkable for size, and hardly grand enough for the chief of an executive wielding authority over a territory nine millions of square miles in extent. The Cabinet is sitting, or we should be introduced to General Grant, always ready to receive English as well as American visitors.

The Treasury is another magnificent building; and on being introduced to the Treasurer of the United States, he kindly gives instructions to have everything shown to us. The several departments are of great interest. Two thousand eight hundred people are here employed in making and sorting the dollar notes. The old notes are sorted, counted, and packed up by

women, some being ladies of good parentage. In
the strong room, I hold in my hand a packet of notes
for four millions, and every facility is afforded us to
inspect everything, short of bringing them away.

The Patent Office is another great building, containing a collection of models unequalled in the
world. A curiosity in its way is a gigantic obelisk to
the memory of Washington, partly erected, and intended to be the highest in existence. It is already
carried up to a height of two hundred feet, and to complete it another four hundred feet are to be added; it
is not, however, being proceeded with, owing to want
of funds.

Taking the car to George Town, we cross by the
bridge over the Potomac to Arlington, formerly the
residence of General Lee. This estate was forfeited
to the government; and beneath the turf, on the hill
side, lie sixty thousand Confederate soldiers, who fell
in the war for the Union.

Marriages take place of an evening, and we see
what may fairly be called a fashionable wedding at
half-past seven. The ceremony only occupies ten
minutes; the service, what there is of it, resembling
ours, but much curtailed. The party are in evening
dress—bridesmaids in full ball costume, and men in
claw-hammer coats and white chokers, with shoes
heavily rosetted.

A favourite excursion here, and of which we avail ourselves, is a run of eighteen miles by steamer down the Potomac river; a charming line of scenery down both banks, the trees growing to the water's edge. Although a hundred and fifty miles from the mouth, the river is more than two miles wide. Our destination is Mount Vernon, on which stands the late residence of Washington, surrounded by wooded grounds, and, through openings in the trees, commanding beautiful views of the river in both directions. Several relics, including his sword, uniform, despatches, &c., are exhibited, and his tomb in the grounds, in which can be seen his sarcophagus. The steamer runs daily, and is much patronized by visitors to Washington.

We had intended seeing Richmond, but our landlord informs us it is only a one-horse country town; the fortifications once so grand, being now all erased by the plough. So we conclude it is hardly worth while to go a hundred miles out of our way to see it, as we can go direct from here to our next destination Gordonsville, where we are to spend a few days with a relative settled there, who will then accompany us on our journey westward. We accordingly leave by early morning train from Alexandria (Washington), by the Washington City, Virginia Midland, and Great Southern Railway, for Gordonsvillle, distant eighty-nine miles.

CHAPTER VIII.

VIRGINIA AND THE WHITE SULPHUR SPRINGS.

NEAR GORDONSVILLE—QUIET FARMING—A CORN
SHUCK MATTRESS—REAL THUNDERSTORMS—
INSECTS AND BIRDS—COLOURED LABOUR—
THE ALLEGHANY MOUNTAINS—LIFE AT
THE SPRINGS.

GORDONSVILLE is a junction station, and one would consequently suppose, of some importance. Such, however, is not the case, it being an insignificant little town, if, indeed, it have any claim to that title. Meeting our host at the station, we lumber out in an obsolete United States mail carriage to his farm, about three miles distant. The trap is so decrepit, and the roads so unkind, that even with a pair of horses the journey occupies an hour. We pass a few houses on the way, all timber; and, on arriving, find we are fairly in the heart of the country.

Standing on a gentle rise from the road, is the house, a framed one, of only two floors. The lower, or ground floor, is devoted to the kitchens and offices, cellars, &c.; while the upper floor, approached from without by broad flights of steps to the verandahs, running back and front, contains the sitting and sleeping apartments: the advantage of the two verandahs being, that one is always shaded from the sun. All the rooms communicate with the verandah by outer doors; there is also a staircase inside the house. The building is entirely of wood, on a foundation of brick; the roof is covered with pieces of tough wood, shaped like tiles, called shingles. I give this description, it being the general plan of the houses in the South.

Situated near the Blue Ridge and South West Mountains, the scenery around is gloriously picturesque, much of Virginia being in a wild state of nature. Coming hither in the rail, we noticed thousands and thousands of acres that had never felt the plough or been tickled by a hoe. I have since seen a statement, that of the twenty-six millions of acres in Virginia only six millions are cultivated. This, if correct, is surprising, considering that land can be purchased very cheaply, and with the immense advantage of being near the railways communicating with all the Atlantic cities. It is a fertile country, and produces heavy crops of corn (maize) and wheat. The pastures are rich, and cattle a paying speculation, as also horses and mules.

We find the heat here excessive, and we pass the daytime in a rocking chair under the shade of the verandah or lounging under the thick trees by which the house is surrounded.

The farms here are all worked by coloured labour, and the negroes appear to be unaffected by the heat, as they plough steadily on in the sun with the thermometer at one hundred and forty-five degrees, the only noticeable effect on them being an extra polish.

In the evening darkness comes on very suddenly, when we see hundreds of fire-flies twinkling among the trees with great brilliancy; and, whilst playing whist, we see our first mosquitoes. My first nights on a mattress stuffed with corn shucks are anything but enjoyable, its rugged surface making great impressions on me, while between three and four, when daylight arrives, the flies swarm in and perform on everything human, annoying us greatly.

Whilst here we witness some tremendous thunderstorms, with sheets of water falling. One night especially, whilst we watch the storm from the verandah, the whole sky is aflame with the lightning, the mountains and valleys around being alternately brilliantly illuminated and plunged into darkness impenetrable.

Sunday is smoking hot, and having been well bitten in the night by some playful insects, I do not feel equal to a journey of three miles to hear the local sky-pilot hold forth, but amuse myself by watching the insects, which are innumerable, both great and small. The wood, or carpenter, bees are here in crowds, larger than our humble bees, and very destructive, as they will drive a hole half an inch in diameter through a door or post as cleanly as an auger; cockchafers, and the largest moths and butterflies imaginable. The tobacco moth measures from five to six inches across, and has four transparencies in the wings. There are many birds, amongst which I must notice the robin, like ours in plumage and red breast; it is as large as a full-sized thrush. The great turkey buzzard, wheeling round the tall trees above our heads, is the great scavenger of the country. A dead horse or sheep attracts his notice, and his bones are picked clean within forty-eight hours of his death. The state laws prohibit the slaying of buzzards, and, indeed, they are not worth the shooting, being alive with maggots half-an-hour after.

Altogether, this part of the country is doubtless very

beautiful, and for one who has a taste for quiet farming most enjoyable. In winter the temperature is not excessively cold, and throughout the year there are none of those violent extremes of climate which render the Northern States and Canada to some people almost unendurable.

The day for our departure has arrived, and we have to push our way westward, and as we enter the carriage the darkies cluster round, wishing us good-bye, and bowing to the very ground, at the same time shouting out to our host, now off with us : " Be sure and come back to us, sar." He speaks highly of the negroes as farm labourers ; they certainly appear willing to do anything, and keenly appreciate a kind word and being treated as human beings. They are a merry crew, easily satisfied, and always on the grin.

Jeff rushes on to open the gate—this is the boy, full name Jefferson Davis, who does everything in general and nothing in particular—and we are once more on the move.

Leaving Gordonsville by the Chesapeake and Ohio Railroad, we journey westward, and twenty-one miles distant pass the University of Virginia, at Charlottesville, and stopping at many minor stations come thirty-nine miles farther on to Staunton, the chief English settlement in this State, a thriving town of some age, and possessing many attractive residences and more than one State hospital. We are still travelling onwards, through some really magnificent mountain scenery. The mountains are thickly wooded, and gay with the wild azaleas in full bloom. A tempting place for picnics in appearance, the only drawback being that the rattlesnakes have not only formed the same opinion, but acted upon it, attaching themselves to the freehold, and colonising these woods in earnest.

The last part of our day's journey lies through the Alleghanies, at a great elevation, and we obtain some superb views. It grows quite cold as the sun goes down, and when we arrive at the White Sulphur Springs, ninety-six miles from Gordonsville, and have supplied ourselves with the necessary "creature comforts," we are glad to smoke our cigars round a blazing wood fire.

This fashionable resort of Southern society, during the latter part of the summer and autumn months, is most romantically situate in a kind of bason among the tops of the Alleghany mountains. In the midst of some handsomely timbered greenswards, stands a huge hotel, in which the visitors from all parts congregate at the several meals, and also at the ball given every evening.

Fringed round the edge of the green are more than a hundred little cottages, tastefully designed and buried in foliage, in which the different families reside; the hotel itself accommodating some hundreds of people besides, all forming part of the same establishment. The dining hall seats twelve hundred guests, while the ball and drawing rooms are on an appropriate scale.

In the centre of the grounds is a pavilion, in which a band plays at intervals; and in a kind of temple is the White Sulphur Spring, reputed to possess great medicinal value, the water of which is swallowed with a persistency only equalled by its offensive smell and flavour, which, to say the least, are unmistakeably pungent.

There are also pistol galleries and bowling alleys for those that way inclined, while through the grove on the side of the hill overlooking the river, are winding paths and secluded spots, respectively designated as the Lovers' Walk, the Lovers' Leap, the Lovers' Rest, Courtship Maze, Hesitancy, Rejection, Acceptance, and The Way to Paradise. A lengthy ramble through the woods and along the river's side much delights us; we do not, however, penetrate the brushwood growing up the sides of the mountains, not wishing to disturb the bears and snakes.

CHAPTER IX.

OHIO RIVER AND CINCINNATI TO ST. LOUIS.

WEST VIRGINIA—KANAWHA RIVER—NIGHT ON THE OHIO—NEGRO MELODIES—PORKOPOLIS—INDIANA AND ILLINOIS—HEAT AND DUST—THE GREAT STEEL BRIDGE.

OUR next run is a hundred and ninety miles, by the same line of railway, through the State of West Virginia, the route for about a hundred miles lying alongside the Kanawha river. The rocks and cascades are numerous and wild, while the turns in the road of the mountain passes through which we travel afford frequently changing views, the verdure above forming a rich setting to the foam of the tumbling and tossing waters below.

Arriving in the afternoon at Huntington, on the Ohio river, we take the steamer "Fleetwood" for

Cincinnati, a hundred and sixty miles distant. We are now in the heart of the old slave fields—the home of the negro. On one side of the river is Ohio, on the other Kentucky, with hills on either side, and foliage to the water's edge.

A magnificent night follows a burning day; the moon appearing a crescent of silver, and the stars like jewels. Sitting near the head of the vessel on the upper-deck, we can fully appreciate the quiet beauty of the scene, the only sound being the rippling of the water against our sharp bow, and the dull rapid thuds of the paddle floats as we shoot along over the dark still waters. Later on, a number of darkies below sing some plaintive ditties in capital unison, and quite appropriately complete the picture.

Occasionally stopping at some wayside villages, we speed on through the night, and come on deck in the early morning to find an entire change of scene: trees and country have disappeared, and we are lying alongside the wharf, extensive manufactories and boat building yards hard by, while on the Kentucky bank of the river are large towns opposite.

We have arrived at Cincinnati, nicknamed Porkopolis, from its enormous trade in pork and bacon, for which it is the principal mart in the States—a rough and ready kind of place after what we have seen. Its commerce is extensive, and its railroad connections in all directions render it a great trade centre. It also boasts one of the largest inland populations.

The great suspension bridge over the river attracts our attention, and the public buildings are numerous, but need no special comment; like all thriving American cities, it boasts its three or four parks and handsome cemetery.

There is not much here to induce a long stay, and we leave in the early morning by a parlour car of the Ohio and Mississippi railway, fitted with easy chairs, for a journey of three hundred and forty miles to St. Louis. We have a long day's run through Indiana, stopping at Vincennes twenty minutes for dinner; leaving here, we are delayed a few miles away by the engine giving out, another having to be sent for, in consequence of which we lose about an hour, although we put on a great pace to make it up if possible.

The latter part of the route lies through Illinois, a flat country, the dust proving a perfect scourge, as it comes through everywhere; and that, combined with the thermometer at ninety-five degrees, makes us appear truly pitiable objects on our arrival,—the dust and perspiration together having tinted our collars a delicate fawn colour.

Glad are we to alight from the train after a ride of more than thirteen hours, and enter the omnibus for the Southern Hotel, crossing the Mississippi by the great steel bridge, another American wonder. It has three spans of five hundred and twenty-six feet, with a double track for railways under the roadway, and cost ten million dollars.

CHAPTER X.

THE QUEEN, OF THE MISSISSIPPI.

ST. LOUIS—SUGGESTED SEAT OF THE GOVERNMENT—
LAFAYETTE PARK—BASE BALL—SUNDAY IN
ST. LOUIS—THE SIX SHOOTER.

ST. LOUIS, capital of the State of Missouri, and upwards of a thousand miles west of New York, stretches for some distance along the west bank of the great Mississippi, and is the centre of all the trade and navigation of that river; the numbers of steamers lying alongside the wharves being a sight to remember. Steamers ply from here up the river to St. Paul or down to New Orleans, and carry many passengers and much merchandise. The river itself is not pellucid, but, on the contrary, is of a thick and muddy appearance. The banks are low, and the surrounding country as flat as the Essex marshes.

Its railway connections are manifold, and extend like a network in every direction. It has often been suggested that this should be the seat of the Government, as being the most central city, and consequently more convenient. Beyond the mere suggestion, however, nothing has transpired towards carrying it into effect, and, although we cannot tell what time may effect in in such a country, at present there would seem but little prospect of its accomplishment, or of the magnificent city of Washington, with its princely public buildings and offices, erected at a cost of many millions sterling, being vacated.

Extending for a considerable distance, and containing a population of half a million, St. Louis appears almost crowded, the streets being always filled with a busy, bustling throng. The public buildings are numerous, the stores well kept, and everything bright and attractive, especially at night. Concert rooms abound, as well as billiard saloons and drinking bars, all of which are well patronised.

It also possesses several parks, of which I may mention Lafayette, about two miles out. Small, but prettily laid out, it has an ornamental lake with fountains, on which are pleasure boats, their prows fashioned after the head and neck of the swan; and statues of Benton, and I need hardly add Washington, adorn the grounds.

A good swimming bath here proves as acceptable as it is uncommon. Ample in size, with a depth of eight-

and-a-half feet, it leaves nothing to be desired. The art is being encouraged here, and gold medals presented for competition. I notice this, as the lack of swimming baths throughout, even in towns situated on the banks of a river or lake, much surprised us.

At Grand Avenue Park, outside the city, we witness a grand match at base ball, St. Louis *versus* New York. A large concourse of spectators are present, and evince great enthusiasm over every successful hit or catch. After some spirited play the St. Louis men win the match, amid much cheering.

St. Louis has the reputation of being a gay, fast, and wicked city; certainly it wears a very different aspect to saintly Boston or Quaker Philadelphia. Sunday here is of a Parisian pattern; the stores all open, the new piece at the theatre commences to-night, and a grand match at base ball to be played this afternoon. Two long processions of the Good Templars have been parading the streets, with banners and mounted bands, and the whole city appears to be *en fête*.

Apparently a spirit of lawlessness increases as we go West. I notice many here are armed, and at the bars, and even in the hotels, the many-barrelled revolver is ever present. I think the American eagle should be pourtrayed with a six-shooter in his claw: he is incomplete without.

CHAPTER XI.

MISSOURI, KANSAS, AND COLORADO.

GRASSHOPPERS—KANSAS CITY—THE PLAINS—SHARP EATING—THE TRAPPER AND THE INDIANS—THE BOUNDLESS PRAIRIE—BUFFALOES—PRAIRIE DOGS AND JACKASS RABBITS.

LEAVING St. Louis by the St. Louis, Kansas City, and Northern Railway, we cross the River Missouri, twenty-two miles down, by the great iron bridge at St. Charles, one mile and a quarter in length, and pass through some fine lands, the crops of maize and wheat being thick, but in parts much damaged by the grasshoppers, who are flying about in millions. The papers teem with accounts of their terrible depredations, thousands of acres having been laid waste by these destructive insects. They will settle in a cloud on a patch of wheat or corn, and lay it bare in one night. The country seems subject to periodical scourges of this kind. At one time the army worm was its dreaded enemy. The hamlets are few and far between, and with the usual halts for meals, we reach Kansas City late at night, having traversed the whole width of Missouri, from east to west, a distance of two hundred and seventy-five miles.

We put up at Coates' House, a very fair hotel on the hill, and are enlivened by the unmusical croaking of the bull-frogs, in a piece of marshy land nearly opposite. This is an entirely new city, and everything has that uncomfortable appearance when fresh from the hands of the workman. It is admirably placed, and is already taking its place in the chain of great cities stretching across to the west. Already they are doing a great cattle trade here, one firm alone slaughtering twelve hundred beasts daily. The rapid growth of places out here approaches the marvellous—the village becomes a town, and the town swells out into a large city in the space of four or five years, in a way almost magical.

The Kansas Pacific Railway now takes us in hand, and having entered the State of Kansas, we now see the real wildness and solitude of the west. We first traverse the plains, a perfectly level country; and one gigantic field of wheat attracts our notice, and we learn it is the largest in the State, comprising thirteen hundred acres.

We dine at Topeka, the capital—if a meal, which has to be ordered, obtained, and devoured in less than twenty minutes, can be termed dinner. The hurried wolfing of a beefsteak—the national dish—and bolting of other sundries, topped up with an ice and a pint of iced tea, or milk, certainly allays our hunger, and we regain our seats in the train at the cry from the guard of "All aboard," feeling more satisfied than refreshed.

Hour after hour passes by as we rattle on towards the setting sun. We rouse some wild boars, which causes an immediate discharge of revolvers from the carriage windows, the hogs, nevertheless, escaping. Many a league we pass with scarce a habitation. In the smoking carriage I meet three Cornish men, who seem mightily pleased to have a long chat about their beloved county, after many years' absence.

We sup at Salina, and on resuming our journey I have an interesting conversation with a trapper, who lives at the southern portion of Kansas, adjoining the Indian territory, a most dangerous locality. He is now going there, and, being alone, travels by night, for safety's sake; as in the day, unless accompanied and well armed, death is certain, the Indians compassing the end of every white man. He tells me of a young Englishman lately in his employ, who, whilst out with five companions, was captured, only three escaping. He died game, but was horribly tortured; his finger and toe nails being drawn out, his body then gashed all over with knives, and being finally put out of his misery by having his skull cloven in two by a tomahawk. He also informs me, with tears in his eyes, that he lost two of his own boys last year (murdered by the Indians), and deeming the neighbourhood no longer safe, has removed his family to Topeka. Rough in appearance, his rifle slung across his shoulders, he appears the backwoodsman so often described by Cooper, as I wish him a safe journey and bid him God-speed on his alighting at a small wayside station.

Still whirring along all night, we leave the plains and commence crossing the prairie. It is a boundless sea of green, extending to the horizon. Growing from one to two feet in height, the prairie grass is unbroken by a single tree or shrub, and as we rattle along, hour after hour, without the least change of scene, the immense extent of America grows apparent.

We breakfast at Wallace, a solitary eating station, and again go forward. The heat is now one hundred degrees in the cars, proving very oppressive, as we are forced to keep the windows closed to prevent the blacks from the funnel raining in upon us. The fuel is wood, and gives off much smoke, the top of the smoke stack being covered with a wire grating, to secure the live ashes from setting fire to stacks or crops we pass through.

We catch sight of some buffaloes, about half-a-mile distant, with their heavy and unwieldy head and shoulders, ragged mane, and mean hind quarters. Numerous skeletons of these animals are to be seen on each side of the line through the prairie, having been shot down from the passing trains. The prairie dogs here are very numerous. They congregate in groups, called towns, each living in a separate hole in the sand on the top of a small mound. As the train approaches, these inquisitive animals sit up on their hind legs on the top of the mound to see us pass, and this inviting attitude elicits many rounds from our shooting irons, poor doggie having to bite the dust. Some fine antelopes are frequently surprised, and bound away at a wonderful speed. The jackass rabbits also attract our notice. They are very large, and on being disturbed cock their enormous ears like donkeys, and go lurching away in an ungainly fashion.

To watch these different animals, and attempt their destruction, are the chief diversions of the journey, and we are not sorry, when evening approaches, after a ride of eighteen hours and a half, to reach Denver, a distance of six hundred and forty miles from Kansas City.

CHAPTER XII.

DENVER AND THE ROCKY MOUNTAINS.

DENVER—LONG'S AND PIKE'S PEAKS—A WONDERFUL MOUNTAIN CHAIN—UP AMONG THE ROCKIES—BLACK HAWK—CENTRAL CITY—NOVEL GAMBLING—IDAHO SPRINGS—A BURNING FOREST—GOLD DIGGERS—A SLICE OF LUCK—MOUNTAIN SCENERY—TORTURE ON WHEELS—ANOTHER FIRE.

TWO thousand miles from New York, we are now fairly in the far West. Lying at the base of the Rocky Mountains, Denver, the capital of Colorado, is a fast rising city, and the centre of the several mining districts. It is situated on the plain, the adjacent mountains presenting views of wild grandeur; some clad with thick pine trees, while the snowy range tower in the background. To the northward, Long's Peak, ten thousand feet above the sea, and seventy miles distant, can be plainly discerned; while looming in the distance, eighty miles to the southward, Pike's Peak rears its head to the clouds to a height of more than fourteen thousand feet, the whole forming a view of one grand continuous chain of nearly two hundred miles.

We are greeted on our arrival with another thunderstorm, followed by a gorgeous sunset, which the local press describe the next day as of unusual beauty.

This city covers an immense extent of ground, and most of the streets are planted with trees; the pavements are planked, and the buildings are quite new. This place has become of importance only during the last five years, in which time it has increased fourfold.

Having resolved to see something of the interior of the Rocky Mountains before resuming our course westward, we accordingly travel by the Colorado Central Railroad to Black Hawk, a distance of thirty-nine miles. The first town we reach is Golden City, at the commencement of the range. The last twenty-two miles of this line has a guage of only three feet, and yet travels with perfect safety. We now enter the mountains, and run alongside the mountain torrent. Creeping slowly along the side of the mountain, a precipitous wall of rock overhanging, we view the roaring water on the other side, leaping over great masses of rock, varied occasionally by a splendid waterfall. It is considered the most extraordinary piece of railway engineering in the world, and they say here, proves that no mountain is inaccessible to the railway constructor. It takes us three hours to accomplish the journey, when we alight at Black Hawk, a mining town, at an altitude of seven thousand eight hundred feet. Within the last seventeen years, gold has been extracted in this spot to the amount of nearly a million sterling.

The stage from the railway takes us up a steep road to Central City, a mile distant, and we are now eight thousand three hundred feet up on the Rocky Mountains (or about the same height as the St. Gothard Pass over the Alps), and put up at the Teller House.

Built irregularly along the side of the mountain, a terribly steep street running through the centre, this city presents no object of beauty, but is interesting on account of its extraordinary position. It is peopled with miners, the country round being literally riddled with gold mines.

We notice here a novel form of gambling. Against the wall of a gallery are fastened photographic portraits (cartes de visite), to the number of some four or five hundred. Behind some a certain amount is inscribed, from ten dollars downwards, with of course many blanks. The speculator pays half-a-dollar, and may select any picture he pleases, which is then removed by the proprietor, and the amount, if any, paid over. It is patronized by the miners, whom we watch playing and putting down their money without hesitation. One lad, who takes two chances, wins ten dollars, and like a prudent investor at once evaporates, apparently satisfied for this evening.

We climb to the top of the mountains outside the town, and have an extensive view, the air being crisp and clear; a fine golden eagle is soaring overhead, but will not come within range to give us an opportunity of shortening his life.

Leaving Central, we hire a trap and pair to take us to Idaho Springs; and a drive it is. Distant six miles, the road lies along the side of the mountains, now up, now down, now all but tilted out on one side, and then on the other, at times appearing somewhat dangerous. The views, however, are superb; the pines grow up the sides of the mountains to a height of eleven thousand feet, at which line they give it up, and resign all above to the rocks and eternal snow. A grand view of the Old Chief, one of the highest peaks, is also gained on this road; and shortly after a sharp turn brings us all at once into the valley, where is situate the little village of Idaho Springs, and we dismount at the Beebee house, a charming little rustic hotel.

Of all the beautiful spots on this earth I have yet seen, this eclipses all. In a valley of the Rocky Mountains, it appears like a toy village, with its little white frame houses, and a roaring tumbling river rushing through its midst. Around us tower the rugged mountains, some twelve hundred feet above our heads, whilst between them may be seen the snow-clad peaks of others fifty miles away.

The roads are planted with trees, and all is deliciously quiet, the air cool and sweet, and there is a drowsy kind of enchantment about the whole scene that has fairly taken me by storm. Remote from the rest of the world, we can enjoy its silent beauty, after the excitement and bustle of the great Atlantic cities, and the rattle of more than two thousand miles in the cars.

A natural hot spring supplies a large swimming bath, the heat of the water being ninety-five degrees. It flows from the rock even hotter than this. On our road here we saw a burning forest, the smoke rolling for miles. We can still see the smoke in the distance, and it will probably burn for another two or three days. It is not an unusual occurrence in these parts, and a fire will often clear two or three thousand acres of wood.

Whilst here we inspect a gold mine, and see the whole operation down to the panning out. The day's work has realized four ounces of gold, which fetches twenty dollars per ounce. The proprietor employs four hands, who are paid five dollars each per day. He tells us he has been engaged at this occupation for more than twenty years, and likes its excitement. There are several mines up the valleys about here, many not being worked. There have been many instances of good fortune, the following for instance: Near here, three men got out a heap from the mine during cool weather, and washed it out afterwards. The washing occupied them thirty-one days, during which time they averaged six hundred dollars a day, rewarding each man with twelve hundred pounds for less than three months' work from first to last.

We ramble up the valley for a few miles, whipping the stream for trout, but with little luck. Only a few fish, and those of moderate size, fall to our share; but the sun being bright and dazzling, destroys our chance; then, again, the streams, for a distance of five to six miles from any settlement, are fished to death by the miners and inhabitants. The scenery around so wild and desolate, yet strangely beautiful, quite repays our different wanderings, and we are fonder of the spot than ever.

I would remark here, that one of the finest countries in the world for the sportsman exists about fifty miles from here, at Central Park, where big game, such as elk and antelope abound, also smaller animals, and the trout fishing is unsurpassed. Special arrangements have, however, to be made for the purpose; and a tent, with necessary fittings, provisions, and cooking utensils provided, as also a guide knowing the country, together with a mule and cart to carry everything. This is frequently done by a party of three or four, who then go out for a month or six weeks of real sport, camping out and moving on from day to day.

In the cool of the evening, we bathe in the river, and although in most parts extremely shallow, we find the power of its current almost resistless. As night approaches, it much pleases us to sit under the verandah and watch the rising of the moon. The constantly changing effect, as peak after peak is lit up by the rising light, is worth waiting to see; and as the moon is near the full, and the air singularly clear, she shines with unwonted brilliancy.

The few days spent here will not soon be forgotten; and we leave Idaho Springs with much regret for Floyd Hill, whence we rejoin the cars to Denver.

By the stage passing through here once a day, we book outside seats, and start in the afternoon. The distance is five miles, and the scenery, I believe, very grand for those fortunate enough to see it; but, being outside passengers, it takes us all we know to cling to our seats and watch for the ruts and pieces of rock that the coach has to plunge into or jerk over. It is positively dreadful,—the vilest road that man's enemy could devise in his most fiendish humour; narrow also to a degree. We meet some waggons full of hay, drawn by mules, and to let them pass have to draw on one side, my legs hanging over the precipice. On the mule driver cracking his whip, our leaders get skittish, and there seems a very fair prospect of our tour being ended and ourselves concluded among the Rockies. Add to all this a blinding dust, that frequently prevents us seeing even the horses, and our delight may be imagined when the cars are in sight, and we descend, sore and shaken, from this execrated coach. The driver admits it to be one of the worst roads he knows; and a fellow-passenger, who has travelled hundreds of miles through Colorado, has seen nothing like it. Here I conclude, as I am unable to give a perfect description without using bad language.

Again entering the little cars, we wind our tortuous way along apparently inaccessible places, the train running down the incline by its own impetus, steam being shut off, and the speed of the train entirely controlled by the brakesmen. We see another fire, and this time close to us, the pine trees crackling up in a few minutes, and a large boulder, displaced by a falling tree, just striking the train as it bounds into the valley, but fortunately doing no damage.

We notice along this route many Chinamen; they appear to be universally employed as labourers on the railroads out west; and between here and San Francisco are very numerous, especially as waiters at the eating stations.

Returned to Denver, we explore the suburbs, where already large private residences are in course of erection, and many trees of all kinds being planted in the gardens.

It will be a fine city some day or other, but the soil is so dry and horribly dusty, that it can never be pleasant in dry weather.

CHAPTER XIII.

WYOMING, UTAH, AND SALT LAKE CITY.

THE HIGHEST RAILWAY STATION IN THE WORLD—
WAHSATCH MOUNTAINS—ECHO AND WEBBER CANONS
—OGDEN—A SMASH UP—GREAT SALT LAKE—
THE MORMON CITY—THE PROPHET AND
THE GOVERNMENT—A TRAVELLING
CIRCUS.

A HUNDRED and nine miles by the Denver Pacific Railroad, our course lying almost due north from Denver, and we reach Cheyenne, in the State of Wyoming, the junction with the Union Pacific Railroad. Having an hour to spare, we enjoy a good "square meal" before changing into the cars of that line, when we once more roll away across the prairie and enter the Rocky Mountains, crossing the summit at Sherman, altitude eight thousand two hundred and forty-two feet—the highest railway station in the world. Twenty-five miles beyond we halt at Laramie for supper. The night is starlight; as we drive on through the rocks and prairie grass, the scenery round is rugged and desolate, and crossing the Laramie river, we find by morning that we have entered the State of Utah, and pull up at Green River, another eating station, for breakfast. Very picturesque is the scenery here, the river being broad and shallow—the old fording place of the stages, when the journey to Salt Lake City used to be a question of some months, long trains of foot-sore travellers, horses, mules, and bullock waggons dragging wearily along across the prairie and the desert, under a scorching sun, their stout hearts often failing them, together with many of their lives, on their terrible journey to the promised land, which so many were destined never to reach. The dangers of attack from the Indians; sufferings from scarcity of food for themselves and cattle, and want of water; with intrusions at night from wild beasts made bold by hunger, are happily events of the past, and can now hardly be imagined by those enjoying the comfort and luxury of sleeping and drawing-room cars on this wondrous line of railway.

And now we enter upon some of the grandest

scenery in the universe, through the rocks and bluffs of the Wahsatch mountains. Staying at Evanston for dinner, we then travel at a moderate speed through a pass whose scenery is truly remarkable, comprising the Echo and Weber Canons, with Castle and Pulpit Rocks; the One Thousand Mile Tree—exactly that distance from Omaha; the Devil's Slide, a fearfully steep and narrow incline between two natural walls of rock; and Devil's Gate, a wonderful group of rocks; and passing between huge masses of rock on every side, that defy description, we reach Ogden, the termination of this line and commencement of the Central Pacific. This is a Mormon town of some importance, but presenting nothing of striking interest.

A few minutes after leaving the train, we see it run into by another, the two engines meeting and smashing up their cow-catchers, also wrecking one carriage, fortunately clear of passengers. This little excitement over we take the branch line to Salt Lake City, thirty-seven miles south, passing along the shores of the Great Salt Lake.

It resembles an inland sea, being a hundred and fifty miles long and forty wide; the mountains on the opposite side sloping down into the water. Passing several Mormon villages, we reach the Great Mormon City in the evening, after a run of six hundred and fifty-nine miles straight off the reel.

ECHO CAÑON, UTAH.

Located at the Walker House, East Temple Street, we find ourselves in the midst of what a Yankee would call a "bully" city. Seated on the plain it is singularly situated, being entirely surrounded by snow-capped mountains. The streets are all planted with trees, mostly acacias, here called locusts, while bright streams of water rush rapidly along either side. The city's general aspect is clean, quiet, and attractive. Truly the Prophet knew where to pitch his tent.

The Mormons, of course, are pre-eminent, and constitute about two-thirds of the community, the remainder being termed Gentiles, who since the railroad was opened have literally poured in. The stores of the Mormonites may be distinguished by the letters Z.C.M.I. (Zion's Co-operative Mercantile Institution) being placed above them.

The principal building is the Tabernacle, a large oval, with a roof resembling a dish cover minus the handle; it is monstrously ugly, but has good acoustic properties, and seats twelve thousand people. At one end of the gallery are Brigham's seat and pulpit, the former covered by an old buffalo hide; below him sit the twelve apostles, and again under them, the bishops and elders. A fine organ, the woodwork of which is carved with great skill, is noticeable as having been entirely built by the Mormons in Salt Lake.

Prominent round the front of the gallery enclosure

are mottoes and conceits in large type, among which we remark, "United we stand, divided we fall;" "Hail, Brigham, our friend and prophet;" "Utah's best crop, children."

Brigham's residence is of wood, with verandahs, and smaller houses adjoining for his wives; the whole enclosed within a stone wall ten feet high. He has, however, a new residence in course of erection, in the modern French style.

There is also a Temple of granite, intended to be a wonder when completed. As, however, it has been in hand twenty-four years, and is now only fifteen feet above the ground, at a cost of three million dollars, the date of that event, to say the very least, appears remote.

We do not see the Prophet, he being absent on an excursion with some of the Apostles. He is, we learn, fast losing his power here; indeed we find the local papers speaking of him with studied disrespect. It must be remembered that Salt Lake City, as she appears to day, is due to his energy and determination, and that he is naturally looked up to and believed in by his followers in consequence. It is supposed that, though averse to polygamy, the Government will wait until he "passes in his checks," as they term it, before it be abolished altogether. He is now seventy-four years of age, but hale and hearty.

From the summit of a hill on the outskirts, a fine bird's eye view can be obtained. So quiet is every thing, that the city seems to be sleeping in the sunshine, with its houses half-buried in foliage, and the snowy range in the distance; while the great Salt Lake resembles a sheet of silver, without a sail or passing bird to be seen to ruffle its placid surface.

All Salt Lake, nevertheless, turns out in the evening to participate in that sight of sights, the circus. This is periodically looked forward to at all the inlying towns of the States, and every man, woman, and child, whatever be their lot, can always find the requisite dollar for admission. It stays at the towns it visits for a day or two at most; and everywhere we pass through can be seen the trace of its visit in the circle of sand heaped up to make the site.

I must not omit to mention the hot sulphur springs, about two miles out by the tram-car; a good swimming bath is erected, and the temperature of the water the hottest spring we have experienced.

CHAPTER XIV.

THE SIERRA NEVADAS.

THE GREAT DESERTS—INDIANS AND THEIR SQUAWS—
CALIFORNIA — SNOW SHEDS — CAPE HORN —
MARVELLOUS SCENERY—HARVEST TIME—
SACRAMENTO—SAN FRANCISCO BAY.

AGAIN traversing the distance along the branch line to Ogden, we there enter the cars of the Central Pacific Railroad, and proceed along the north side of the Great Salt Lake, and seventy miles beyond enter the Great American Desert, to cross which occupies some hours. Next morning we breakfast at Elko, in the state of Nevada, and dine at Battle Mountain.

We are now in the great Sandy Desert of Nevada, and weary are the hours as we pass over an arid waste of sand and dust, with some little straggling stunted shrubs and a few long withered blades of grass. At the little wayside stations we see many Indians, who have ridden over with their squaws, who ride astride like the men; one Indian being usually attended by half-a-dozen squaws. They are a queer-looking people, and their get-up most ludicrous. The chiefs wear immense earrings, and their complexions are as fresh as paint can make them, which they seem to consider very killing.

Two of them ride with us in the smoking carriage for some distance, and give us an opportunity of closely inspecting them; they are death on beads, and wear them in profusion. They have a very low type of countenance, especially the women, who appear like brute beasts, and carry their papooses, or infants, strapped to a board and slung on to their backs. The men wear their hair very long, and as coarse and thick as a horse's mane, the little children being not much better.

We sup at Humboldt, after which we pass within view of Humboldt Lake, and catch sight of a grizzly out for his evening stroll on the mountain; and at daybreak are in California, commencing the ascent of the Sierra Nevada Mountains. The route is steep and winding, with many snowsheds, of which, altogether, there are about forty miles, these being erected to prevent the line being buried in snow, and in winter forming a tunnel.

We breakfast at Summit—the highest station on this railway—and then begin the gradual descent, through

the most marvellous scenery in the world. It i
impossible adequately to describe it. We creep alon;
the sides of the mountains—where it would seen
impossible for a goat to find standing room—ove
chasms, crossed by timber bridges, of immense height
and when we stop at Cape Horn the view an(
surroundings are simply wonderful.

Perched up on the side of an immense acclivity, w(
gaze from the platform of the car upon a stupendou
mountain, rearing itself up between two valleys.

The valley immediately below us is full of giganti(
pines, which appear like little Christmas trees in th(
distance. From the rail, our car-platform overhangs ;
precipitous descent into the valley, the houses appear
ing like little card boxes down below. When I finc
that we are two thousand feet above them I no longe
wonder at their appearing so tiny, although the)
are distinct, owing to the singular clearness of th(
atmosphere. Mountain peaks stand out clearly ;
hundred and a hundred and fifty miles distant, whil(
sportsmen, new to the country, will often fire at ar
animal a mile away, thinking it about three hundrec
yards.

Beside these Titanic creations of nature, our trair
and passengers indeed appear insignificant, althougl
we cannot but admire the wondrous ingenuity of th(
men who could construct a really safe and substantia

CROSSING THE SIERRA NEVADAS, CAPE HORN.

railway in the face of such difficulties. This portion of the line was made principally by Chinamen, who had first to be suspended by ropes over the side of the mountain to cut a foothold. For many hours we wind along, through the most majestic country. It is admitted to be unsurpassed in the whole world, and, indeed, it were difficult, or rather impossible, to imagine such without actually seeing it. Hundreds of miles of sweeping mountains, clothed with millions of fir trees; now and then a calm, transparent lake, thousands of feet below, the absence of humanity and the wild majesty of nature, uncontrolled since the creation, make up a series of pictures never to be forgotten. Only the brush of a consummate artist could give any idea of such a fabled scene of nature's splendour.

As we descend and draw clear of the Sierras, we find a country revelling in the fullest crops of wheat and corn, vineyards, and occasionally hops. It is harvest-time, and as the weather here is not capricious, but can be relied on, the crops lie upon the ground until all is cut.

At the same time, the country seems terribly burnt up, and the foliage of the trees quite brown; the farms having to be watered by irrigation. The heat becomes intense, and when we reach Sacramento, the capital, almost unbearable. There is a here a great quantity of fruit for sale, the cherries being especially fine. The River Sacramento runs through here, and there is communication with San Francisco by steamer.

The climate of this city bears the reputation of consistency, in being always excessively hot ; it is now upwards of one hundred degrees in the shade ; and we are not sorry when, after a halt of some forty-five minutes, we move on again, passing Stockton, a great wheat mart on the San Joaquin River, and after a journey of nine hundred and twenty miles from Salt Lake City, at last arriving at Oakland, the terminus of the Central Pacific Railroad, an attractive town facing the bay, with many private residences.

The railway runs to the end of a long jetty, the water being very shallow, whence we step on board the steamer to cross the bay, on the opposite side of which, about three miles distant, lies the City of San Francisco.

CHAPTER XV.

THE CITY OF THE GOLDEN GATE.

SAN FRANCISCO—HOTELS—CLIMATE—THE PEOPLE—
SUNDAY—A STREET-PREACHER—SEA-LIONS—THE
PACIFIC OCEAN—THE GOLDEN GATE—WOOD-
WARD'S GARDENS—JOHN CHINAMAN.

SO sudden is the change from the heat of the last two days, to the now really cold evening breeze sweeping across the bay, that we fairly shiver again. The sun has just set behind the mountains, throwing everything into a fitful and uncertain light, and San Francisco fast rising into view, its lights commencing to twinkle out like stars. Situated on an eminence, and sloping down to the sea, Frisco at first sight is very captivating, the numerous fine vessels at anchor making up a striking picture.

We take up our quarters at the Occidental Hotel, Montgomery Street, and have reached the farthest point of our tour, and completed our journey from the Atlantic to the Pacific.

San Francisco is situated on the western side of the bay, and possesses a magnificent land-locked harbour, entered from the Pacific by the Golden Gate. It is now one of the most important ports in the world, and its wealth and commerce immense. Montgomery, California, Kearney, and other principal streets contain many fine buildings and shops. The style of ornament is, however, in many cases overdone and meretricious, and tells of newly-made wealth.

The chief hotels are the Occidental, Lick House Grand, Cosmopolitan, and The Palace—the last-named nearly completed, and to be the largest in the world, is on a gigantic scale. They are all less in their charges than in the Atlantic cities, varying from two and a half to three and a half dollars per day, while everything is on an equally liberal scale.

The climate here is very remarkable, the morning being mild and of a delightful temperature. It only varies about ten degrees in winter. Towards afternoon, however, a bitterly cold wind sets in, blowing up a blinding dust and sand.

Life in the streets here is a study of itself, and one might well be at a loss to tell what part of the world he were in, if suddenly dropped into it.

Great is the confusion of tongues, all nations of the

world being represented—with the consequent variety of costume. There is, however, a smarter dash and spirit about the business men than in New York—and the orthodox city costume and stove-pipe hat are to the front.

We have noticed the clear complexions of the women and children in California : they, as well as the men, appear more robust than the down-easters.

Sunday here is a scene of much gaiety. All Frisco is out in the sunshine—some on their way to the various places of worship (and the City boasts of some fine churches); others attracted by an infidel preacher at the corner of the street, who denounces all religions in most unmeasured terms, and for what is wanting in logic makes up in lung. He clinches his arguments by repeatedly offering to bet five hundred dollars in gold in support of his disbelief, and excites more amusement at his buffoonery than respect for his opinions.

The ladies are out in shoals, well dressed in latest European fashions—in the morning affecting muslin and summer costumes, while in the afternoon, sealskin jackets for the ladies and stout overcoats for the sterner sex are indispensable. The coachmen of the fashionable equipages are also buttoned up to the throat, and the animals themselves enveloped in cloths.

This evening all the streets are fairly crowded; the billiard saloons in full swing, and the various bar keepers busily engaged in serving "whiskies straight," or concocting "fancy drinks," which are gulped down with an avidity almost amusing.

No one visiting San Francisco ever misses seeing the sea-lions. A ride out of some six miles along a splendid road brings us to the Cliff House, from the balcony of which these huge animals can be seen disporting themselves in hundreds on and around the rocks some little distance from the shore below—barking, roaring, and tumbling about as if demented.

A broad belt of golden sand fringes the shore of the Pacific Ocean away to the southward, with a low uneven coast of sand hills; while to our right rise from the water the bold headlands of the Golden Gate, the entrance to the harbour, through which a fine barque has but lately passed, and is some five miles out beating away to the westward.

On our road back to the city we turn aside to ascend Lone Mountain, on the summit of which stands a wooden cross. This is seen far out to sea, and serves as a beacon to vessels entering. From here is obtained a fine view of the Golden Gate and entrance to the bay.

Woodward's Gardens are another place of amusement, and well worth a visit; a combination of Zoo, Aquarium, Museum, and Skating Rink all rolled into one, it is much patronised, the sight of the afternoon being the feeding of the sea lions—one being the largest known; the leaps of the brute from the rock into the water after pieces of fish, with the consequent showers of dirty water dispersed liberally among the on-lookers, being the source of exhaustless merriment to those who escape the douche.

A visit to China Town, the Chinese quarter of the city, is especially interesting, being peopled entirely by that race. The shops are similar to those in Chinese cities, and they also have a joss-house and theatre. They are a patient hard-working people, and according to local report, succeed in whatever they undertake; in fact, to the detriment of the western man, the trades in which they have competed having invariably fallen into their hands. This is mainly owing to their strictly economical and almost penurious habits. They hoard their savings with the fixed resolve of some day returning to the land of their birth, and sacrifice the present for the "good time coming."

Living upon what an Englishman would starve, they also crowd together in their habitations, as closely as sardines in a box.

The food displayed in their provision shops is far from appetising in appearance,—their pet dish, ducks, being split open, spread-eagled, beaten flat, and dried; while other articles of provender are more curious than tempting, and prove the heathen Chinee to be neither proud nor particular in the matter of eating.

Superstition as to great advantages accruing from being buried at home, makes it a general custom with them to send their dead to China for burial—a by no means unsatisfactory cargo for the shipper, a captain who has been in the trade informs me, as double freight is charged; the dead passengers consequently proving more remunerative than the living, and for once putting entirely to shame the old saw of the live dog's superiority to the defunct lion.

Before quitting Frisco we have to select a route to the famous Yo-Semite Valley, the great wonder of the State. Agents of the different lines lie in wait for us, and we are assured that each one in turn is the best.

We select that *viâ* Merced and Snelling, and on departing take the ferry to Oakland, and retrace our way by the Central Pacific Railway as far as Lathrop, whence we change into the Visalia Branch for Merced, where we roost for the night.

CHAPTER XVI.

YO-SEMITE.

SNELLING—DUDLEY'S—CALIFORNIAN DRIVING—
PRACTICAL JOKING BY THE INDIANS—THE
BIG TREES—THE VALLEY—ROCKS AND
WATERFALLS—A SCORCHER.

'TIS a brilliant morning, and, after a hurried meal, we start by the stage, at six to the moment, for our first day's journey towards Yo-Semite. With four horses we jog along over the plain, on a tolerably uneven road, until by mid-day we reach Snelling, our dining place, a pretty little town, once of some importance, but now wearing a broken-down and deserted aspect. Passing through miles of deserted gold diggings, we thump and bang on, until at six P.M. we reach Dudley's—a cottage hotel, with outlying rooms around, everything very rustic and almost *al fresco*. The next morning, at the same hour, we resume our journey in another stage, through some really magnificent scenery, the first part through a forest, whose overhanging foliage screens us from the burning rays of the sun. Getting among the mountains, the skill of the driver becomes something to admire, as we go tearing round corners with only a few inches to spare for the wheels. It appears dangerous, and some have gone over, but we are comforted by the assurance that this seldom occurs, the California Jehu being noted for his particular skill. The way they gallop six horses down the most fearful inclines, over a narrow and uneven mountain road, with a precipice on one side, is something wonderful.

The Indians, to whom Yo-Semite has always been their happy valley and earthly paradise, yet grudge the white man its possession, and still play him practical jokes in the way of firing the trees, that they may fall across the roadway and thus impede the progress of the stage. We pass many of them still smoking, some charred completely through, and gallop over a rough log bridge across a ravine, the timbers of which are actually burning at the time—another piece of dusky mischief.

We halt, and descend from the stage to inspect the grove of big trees, among which are some monsters, the largest being four hundred feet high, with a diameter of thirty feet. They are estimated to be upwards of two thousand years old. The pine trees here are also of immense growth, running up to two hundred and fifty feet.

As we near the entrance to the valley, we notice a peculiar rock, The City of Pekin, so called from its resemblance in shape to the stern of the great Pacific steamer of that name. Entering the valley, we see on our left El Capitan, a perpendicular rock of granite, four thousand feet above us, while on the opposite side is the beautiful waterfall, The Bridal Veil, falling nine hundred and forty feet, and spreading away like a mist towards the bottom.

We put up at The Coulter, a house modest in its acquirements, with sleeping rooms at a short distance still more so; no gaudy colours or painted work to annoy us, the doors and woodwork displaying their natural grain, as they came fresh from the saw—altogether a rustic simplicity that perhaps we do not fully appreciate. A new hotel in its place is to be erected for next season, with additional accommodation.

As this valley has been described so often, and in detail, I shall merely give a general idea of it by stating that it is a flat green valley, some half-mile in width and seven miles in length. The river Merced, fifty to sixty feet wide, flows through its midst, clear as crystal, and with a considerable current from its being the receptacle of the numerous waterfalls with which this spot is surrounded. On either side the valley is walled in by stupendous rocks, mostly perpendicular, and averaging four thousand feet in height. The principal are the South Dome, six thousand feet above the valley; Cloud's Rest, six thousand four hundred and fifty feet; Mount Starr King, five thousand six hundred feet; while the Cap of Liberty, Three Brothers, Three Graces, the Captain, Sentinel, and Cathedral Rocks are all noticeable for peculiarity of form and gigantic proportions.

This wondrous chasm presents an everchanging aspect, with its marvellous waterfalls sparkling in the sunshine, as it falls across them, or plunged into deep gloom when the black thunderclouds loom angrily overhead, and the brilliant flashes of lightning penetrate the darkness of its cavernous recesses, the deep-mouthed thunder roaring through the iron walls of the valley with a majesty truly sublime.

The principal waterfall, and highest known, is the Yosemite. It falls two thousand six hundred and thirty-four feet in three leaps, and as it shakes in the wind, is even extremely beautiful. There are, also, the Sentinel, Vernal, South Fork, and Ribbon falls, the last named being narrow, flat, and wavy, not unlike a ribbon shaken in the air.

There is some very good fishing in this river, and we land a fair quantity of trout from day to day.

SENTINEL ROCK, YO-SEMITE VALLEY.

A capital billiard saloon and refreshment bar is kept here by an Englishman—Mr. Smith. Attached to it are also hot and cold baths, with every modern appliance. Mr. Smith is a man of enterprise, who has done much for the valley, and is, in fact, its presiding genius.

After a week's stay, we once more mount the stage at six A.M., and rattle out of the valley for our two days ride of 87 miles to Merced.

In a blazing sun, six hours' jerking and jumping along the edges of the precipices brings us to the wayside dining-house, where the skin of a bear is hanging up, the animal having been taken in a trap, a short distance off, the day previous. Then on with fresh horses, another five hours to Dudley's, before-mentioned, renewing our ride next morning. The heat is now intense, and the fierce Californian sun makes one feel very low. Again stopping at Snelling for dinner, we find the heat is ninety-eight degrees in the shady room, with well watered floor. Again across the sandy plains; the horses having pails of water administered frequently, which they drink greedily.

The birds sit in the ditches, endeavouring to escape the sun, and some jack rabbits appear quite helpless. It is not uncommon for crows and other large birds to fall dead from the trees with the heat. A hot north wind is blowing, which adds to our discomfort.

Pulling up at a drinking-shop on the plains, to water the horses, the thermometer stands at one hundred and eight degrees in a deeply shaded room, the floor saturated with water.

Arriving at length at Merced, we sup and turn in. The sheets seem to burn us as we touch them, and with windows wide open we sigh for air, but find that when a puff does enter, it comes like the blast of a furnace, only to make us gasp again.

We are up soon after daybreak, and taking the rail from here, rejoin the main line at Lathrop, and are off eastward by the Central Pacific Railroad.

CHAPTER XVII.

OMAHA, CHICAGO, AND DETROIT.

SILVER PALACE AND PULLMAN CARS—NEBRASKA—
OMAHA—JULIUS MEYER—A HEAVY MOVE—THE
NEW CHICAGO—LAKE MICHIGAN—TRADE—
DETROIT—THE RIVER BY MOONLIGHT.

THE Silver Palace cars of this line are well worth the extra charge to the tourist, which is six dollars to Ogden, and eight more for the Pullman car from there to Omaha, the sleeping arrangements being very complete, while the extra space in these cars is very grateful in hot weather. The line being well laid and the speed only moderate, we can read and play whist comfortably. We now pass over the ground before described—the Sierras, the Deserts, &c., and on reaching Ogden change into the Union Pacific, and pursue our way as before until Cheyenne, when we travel over new ground; fortunately a heavy storm ahead of us has laid the dust and cooled the air for hundreds of miles, which makes the journey more endurable; and traversing Nebraska we pass through some splendid crops of wheat and corn, arriving at Omaha, the capital of that State, after an unbroken run of nearly nineteen hundred miles, five days and four nights in the cars.

Our hotel is The Grand Central. We much enjoy a good bath and a dinner at our leisure, after eating at "lightning express" rate, and stroll about this pleasant city, viewing the river Missouri, and the great iron bridge by which we shall cross it when leaving. From the hills around a good view of this city is obtained, with its two long and straight principal thoroughfares.

We pay a visit to the store of Julius Meyer, with whom we have some conversation. He is a great man with the different Indian tribes, mixing much with them, and understanding their language perfectly. He acted as interpreter, and accompanied the four chiefs who interviewed the President at Washington. His store is a museum of curiosities, not only of Indian manufacture, which naturally are numerous, but also from China and Japan.

Here we behold what we have often heard and read of, but never had the pleasure of witnessing. In the principal street, a full-sized house and store is being moved bodily, to take its place on the opposite side of the road. It is a work of some magnitude, but is of frequent occurrence; a framework being placed beneath the house piece by piece, and when firmly secured, the whole is worked gradually along on rollers, to its new position.

With the thermometer at one hundred degrees in the shade, we jump into our Pullman at Council Bluffs, for a twenty-five hours' run of four hundred and ninety three miles, through the States of Iowa and Illinois to Chicago.

Chicago, Illinois, whose destruction by fire in 1871 was almost complete, and called forth such world-wide sympathy and assistance, now shows but little trace of that awful disaster, except in the blackened ruins of some of the churches not yet rebuilt, and vacant spaces where once stood buildings. The rebuilding of the city has been carried out with an energy and speed truly astounding, and the palatial buildings of every kind, its magnificent hotels, immense commercial stores and elevators, testify to the determination of its people to have once more one of the finest cities of the age, and in fact far handsomer than before. The hotels are vast and sumptuous; the Grand Pacific, Palmer House, Sherman House, and Gardner being the principal. They have all been rebuilt since the fire, and finished with great completeness at a lavish outlay.

The chief streets, Michigan and Wabash Avenues, Clark, and State streets, run parallel with the Lake, and are intersected at right angles, on the usual American system, by Jackson, Madison, Washington, &c.

The city lies at the south of Lake Michigan, on the western side; and the walk and drive by the lake, extending a considerable distance, is a favourite rendezvous. Many private residences overlook the water, which, in appearance, resembles the sea. We had expected to be almost roasted alive here, and are agreeably disappointed to find the temperature enjoyable. A fine breeze is blowing, and quite a sea rolling in. A large vessel has just been wrecked, and a steamer, some three or four miles out, appears to be making a bad time of it.

Some fine churches adorn the suburbs, but not worthy of any special notice. A great number of handsome carriages, well horsed, display on the fashionable drive, and all around are tokens of considerable wealth.

Judging from the piles of warehouses and business premises, foundries and factories, extending right and left for a considerable distance, the numerous railway depôts and termini of the many lines running from here, with the shipping in the port and river, the trade of Chicago must be enormous.

Another severe thunderstorm here one evening, quickly clearing the streets, the whole city brilliant with the lightning, which is unceasing. We see nothing like this in England—the rain falling in rivers of water, and continuing all night.

Leaving our comfortable quarters at the Grand Pacific Hotel, a journey of nine and a half hours, by the Michigan, Central, and Great Western Railway, through Michigan, the first part of the route running near the Lake, of which we catch frequent glimpses, brings us to Detroit, distant from Chicago two hundred and eighty-four miles.

Detroit, largest city in Michigan, is on the Detroit river, connecting Lakes Erie, St. Clair, and Huron. We are quartered at the Russell House, in the centre of the city, facing the City Hall, a noble building, surmounted by a handsome clock tower. In the square is a memorial monument to the war of '61.

Detroit is a beautiful city with very wide streets. The great prevalence of trees in the side streets, with small parks and grounds, give an air of refinement not often met with.

The city extends for some distance, facing the river. In the evening, with a bright moon shining, the scene on the water is worth witnessing, numerous white steamers, carrying many lamps, ferrying to various places. There is music on board to enliven the trip; and we cross over to Windsor, to have our first peep at Canada, that town being situate on the opposite bank.

CHAPTER XVIII.

NIAGARA.

THE NEW SUSPENSION BRIDGE—AMERICAN FALL—
GOAT ISLANDS AND THE RAPIDS—THE HORSE SHOE—
WHIRLPOOL RAPIDS—THE GREAT WHIRLPOOL—
GONE OVER—THE BURNING SPRING—
BATTLEFIELDS AND MONUMENTS.

LEAVING Detroit by the Great Western Railway, we cross the Detroit river, the train running on to an enormous ferry boat, whence we head away to the Canadian terminus at Windsor, from there passing through some very quiet, English-looking country, and staying at London, an important town, for refreshment; next Paris, with its manufactories; and later on, to Hamilton, at the extreme end of Lake Ontario; the fort, with two or three white ships lying off the town, appearing very picturesque.

With a passing glance at St. Catherine's, a pretty little town noted for its mineral springs, and much frequented in consequence, its tinned spires glittering in the sun, we arrive at Niagara Falls. Our baggage passed by the Customs, we drive off to the Clifton House Hotel, on the Canadian side, the position of this house being unequalled—facing the river and commanding a complete view of both the Falls.

These marvellous waterfalls have been described by so many, and have furnished a theme for the rhapsodies of the poet and enthusiasm of the artist, that one fairly stands aghast at the idea of giving a description at all adequate to this marvellous piece of nature's handiwork, unique, even amongst the grandest waterfalls extant.

Staying here for a few days—the only way properly to appreciate the many wonders of the Falls and surroundings—we view them in every way we can suggest.

The river is crossed by a suspension bridge, for horse and foot traffic, a beautiful structure, light as a spider's web and of great span. The towers at either end—one flying the Union Jack, the other the Stars and Bars—can be ascended, and a good general view of the river below and country round obtained. Crossing the bridge, we are again in the States, and go close to the edge of the American fall, a thousand feet wide, and are awed by the sight of such a mass of water rushing over the edge to plunge headlong one hundred and sixty feet into the river below.

NIAGARA FALLS.

Goat Island is reached by a wooden bridge, the boiling rapids roaring along under our feet.

We cross several smaller bridges, over the different rapids, tearing along on their way to the Fall, until we reach the edge of the Horse Shoe.

This fall is two thousand feet wide, and in the shape indicated by its name. The body of water sweeping over the edge is terrific. The spray from below rises up like smoke, to a height of two-hundred-and-fifty feet, while the thunderous roar of the water shakes the air.

The Three Sisters, three little islands above the Falls, and connected by small wooden bridges, afford a magnificent scene of the upper rapids. To see the water coming towards us, it appears that everything must be swept bodily away. As far as the eye can reach, some miles to the horizon, there is nothing but water leaping into the air, as it meets rocks or fallen trees in its furious progress, and it would seem that the ocean had broken its bounds, and is hurrying onwards, bent on the destruction of the world.

A glorious scene presents itself as three rainbows throw their gorgeous colours over the Falls, while the background of rich forest trees of deep green make the foaming waters appear like huge white masses of snow. A weird kind of fascination creeps over the spectator as he gazes on the superb but awful beauty of these world-wondered-at waters. They are altogether beyond description, and must be seen to obtain any idea of their grandeur.

It is curious, meanwhile, to notice the waters, which have raged for miles, until they reach the precipice over which at last they must plunge; and to observe when that final bound is taken, how calmly still the river is below. Gliding slowly but noiselessly along, perfectly smooth, without a ripple on its surface, the only signs of the giant uproar that has found quiet in its deep bosom are the great streaks of foam that lie helplessly on the surface.

Another wondrous point is the view of the Fall from the Canadian side. Of a deep green colour, its surface smooth as glass, the water slips over in a body twenty feet in thickness. One feels his own insignificance standing by these Falls, when he learns that one-and-a-half million tons of water pass over into the river below every minute, and that this Titanic flow has never ceased, night or day, since it was first discovered.

Following the course of the river, some two miles below the Falls, we come to the Whirlpool Rapids, their noise telling us of their whereabouts before we can see them. Here the river rushes through a deep gorge, with precipitous sides, at a rate of twenty-five miles an hour, its waves leaping twenty and thirty feet into the air. The united waters of Lakes Erie, Michigan, and Superior having passed over the Falls, are here compressed into a width of three hundred feet, on their way to join the waters of Lake Ontario, and thence down the St. Lawrence to the Atlantic.

A mile beyond, in a sharp turn of the river, almost at right angles, lies the Great Whirlpool, and here is cast up whatever goes over the Horse Shoe Fall. At the bottom of the American Fall are sharp pointed rocks, and the bodies of the unfortunates who have met their fate at that spot are not recovered, being driven deep into the rocks, and held there by the force of the water.

Walking along the precipitous river bank, we observe many notice-boards affixed to the trees at intervals, informing us "Here four men fell over," "Here Miss ——— jumped over," with other records of various unhappy victims to these waters; and there naturally are occasional accidents of a sad nature. A day or two after our departure we learned that a lady and her lover, while inspecting the Cave of the Winds, slipped on the slimy rocks, and were both swept away into the American Fall.

The Burning Spring, about a mile and a half above the Falls, is a very singular natural wonder. The spring is in a kind of well, and bubbles up with great noise. On a light being held over the surface, the gas liberated from the water ignites; and a gas pipe, on a wide mouthed cylinder, being plunged in, a constant stream of flame continues burning, and appears very extraordinary.

An interesting drive, a short distance out, brings us to Lundy's Lane and Chippewa, the field of a celebrated battle, where the English and Indians fought side by side.

From the top of the General Scott Tower we gain an extensive view of the surrounding country, which is pretty, but somewhat level, with General Brock's monument seven miles distant.

The tourist is amply repaid if he sojourn here for a few days, as it enables him to see the Falls, and really become acquainted with their different characteristics. By moonlight they are also of exceeding beauty, and a ramble along the banks for a few miles above, gives some romantic views of the rapids. A descent should also be made to the rocks on the beach below the Falls, where their height can be appreciated.

Quitting this most interesting spot, we take the rail, fourteen miles to Niagara village, whence the steamer "Rothesay Castle" runs across Lake Ontario. A fresh breeze is blowing, the lake covered with white horses, appearing like the sea, and a delightful run of three hours brings us alongside the landing stage at Toronto.

THE THOUSAND ISLANDS.

CHAPTER XIX.

TORONTO, THE ST. LAWRENCE, AND MONTREAL.

A LONG STREET — THE CITY — LAKE ONTARIO — KINGSTON AND PRESCOTT — ST. LAWRENCE RIVER — THE THOUSAND ISLANDS — SHOOTING THE RAPIDS — VICTORIA BRIDGE — MONTREAL — A GREAT CHURCH — L'ILE ST. HELÈNE — OVERLADEN.

THIS city lies on the north shore of Lake Ontario and is very populous. The streets are well laid out, Yonge Street being the longest thoroughfare in the world, extending as a drive for thirty-five miles in a straight line. The hotels are good; the principal being the Rossin House and Queen's. We stay at the former, situated at the corner of King Street, the chief business thoroughfare.

There are some fine churches and public buildings, the most prominent being the University of Toronto, situate in the Park, and the Law Courts.

There is not the life and activity here we have seen in the cities of the States, the difference being very striking. The streets are quiet, and trade appears to be slack.

There are several theatres, at one of which we twice see the London favourite, Mr. C. Fechter, in "No Thoroughfare" and "The Lady of Lyons," who displays the same power and vigour as of old.

Sunday in Canada is observed considerably stricter than in England. The public-houses are closed, and even tobacconists incur a penalty if carrying on their trade on that day.

We experience, throughout Canada, a grateful change in the temperature, which averages seventy degrees in the shade.

With a beautiful sky overhead, we leave here by one of the Royal Mail Line Steamers for Montreal, and steam down Lake Ontario, keeping within three or four miles of the northern shore. We carry many passengers, causing a great rush for meals and a dearth of state rooms. There is ample room, however, on the decks, from which we enjoy the views of the several waterside towns we call at; the two principal being Kingston, the former capital of Canada, an old town strongly fortified, at the entrance to the St. Lawrence River; and Prescott, the point of debarkation for Ottawa, the capital of the Dominion

LACHINE RAPIDS, ST. LAWRENCE RIVER.

and seat of the Government, whose great features of interest are the Houses of Parliament and Government Offices, which are said to be magnificent. It can be reached by rail or boat up the Ottawa river. We do not visit Ottawa, but proceed on our course down the river St. Lawrence, passing through the romantic scenery of the Thousand Islands. There are in reality some eighteen hundred of them, and as we pick our way between, we get many and varied pictures. The islands are thickly wooded and rocky, of every size and shape, and covered with varieties of foliage.

The latter part of the journey is of an exciting nature, as we shoot several rapids. At parts of the river there is a great fall, and the water rushes madly and wildly along at the rate of twenty miles an hour. The boat rolls and plunges as if in a heavy sea, which the river here resembles. The last and most celebrated are the Lachine Rapids. We take Baptiste, the Indian pilot, on board, at an Indian village a few miles above the Rapids, and he is our man at the wheel. Steam is shut off as we are swept along in the full fury of the tide, and everything is dependent upon the helm. At one time we appear bound to strike on a table of sunken rock, but with a sudden swerve glide by clear, and are once more in still water.

The steamers travel up stream by a canal passing through many locks.

As we approach our destination, we obtain a fine view of the Victoria Tubular Bridge, built by Robert Stephenson, on the same principle as that over the Menai straits. It is a mile and three-quarters long with the abutments, and is a wonder.

Passing beneath it, the city of Montreal lies before us, with quite a forest of shipping, and we run alongside the stage, where several other white river steamers are lying.

Montreal is the largest and most thriving city in Canada, and the chief commercial centre of the British Dominion. It faces the river St. Lawrence, while in its rear rises the mountain Mont Royale, from which it derives its name.

Many fine buildings adorn this city, the streets of which possess handsome shops. The French element here almost preponderates, there being a large population of that race, and their influence increasing. The Roman Catholic cathedral is the largest church in Canada, and seats ten thousand people, the ornamentation and gilding of the interior being profuse. A fine organ and choir of one hundred voices assist in making the service a grand one.

A noticeable feature with the churches are their spires, which are covered with tin, as a protection against lightning; some of the highest roofs are also clothed with that metal, and in the sunshine glitter like silver. We pay a visit to L'Ile St. Helène, a pretty wooded island, given to the people as a park, and reached by the ferry. Thousands avail themselves of it on Sunday afternoons, when the island presents the appearance of a vast pic-nic.

We also cross from the island to Longueil, in what I advisedly term a small boat, to visit a friend resident there. The width of the river on this side of the island is some three-quarters of a mile, and we are not altogether sorry to reach the other side, as our craft is down almost to the water's edge with the four of us, and every ripple of an inordinate size slops playfully into the boat. Fortunately we are free from any passing steamer, or its gentle influence would probably persuade us to swim for it.

We return in the evening by the ferry-boat, crowded to excess with pleasure-seekers, also horses and carriages, and alighting just opposite the island have a long walk to our hotel, the St. Lawrence Hall, passing through a miniature Champs Elysées.

A drive round the city and outskirts to the mountain gives us a good idea of Montreal's position, and affords some extensive views.

CHAPTER XX.

QUEBEC.

GENERAL APPEARANCE—A FORSAKEN CITADEL—THE FORT—HEIGHTS OF ABRAHAM—FALLS OF MONTMORENCY—AN INDIAN VILLAGE—UP THE ST. LAWRENCE—JIGS AND REELS.

THE Grand Trunk Railway of Canada brings us from Montreal, crossing the Victoria Bridge and through some pine-clad country, to Levi's Point in seven hours, whence we ferry across the St. Lawrence to Quebec.

The appearance of this famous city from the water is most imposing—a tall rock crowned by the citadel and forts—and brings to memory "Lionel Lincoln," with Cooper's description of the city, the scene of the tale.

The town is in two parts—The Upper, and Lower, and the streets very steep.

Three-fourths of the population are French, most

of the streets being Rue, &c., while French names over the shop fronts are almost universal.

Everything appears very old and behind the age. Having seen so many brand-new cities possibly makes it strike us more forcibly. The streets are narrow and irregular, the houses old and somewhat picturesque, the churches innumerable—Roman of course prevailing. The general appearance of the city is that of one that once was great, but whose grandeur and vitality are fading away. The removal of the British troops, in '71, has made a great difference to the life of the place. Before that time there were usually quartered here two regiments of infantry and one or two batteries of artillery. The townspeople find the difference both in its gaiety and also the influx of money, which they now miss.

There are only about a hundred men of the Canadian artillery now in garrison, and the splendid citadel, over which we were shown by a corporal, seems almost deserted.

The view from the fort, which is the favourite promenade of an evening, is most exquisite. Three hundred feet above the river, we can see the mountains fifty miles away, and this noble river stretching away for miles, to our right inland, to our left seawards. Several stately ships are at anchor below us, one of the Allan Line ready to sail on the morrow; we watch them and the little white ferry steamers darting backwards and forwards till the sun sets and the lights are run up, when we turn hotelwards.

Near here, within a short drive, are the heights and plains of Abraham, where, a century ago, was fought the memorable engagement between Wolfe and Montcalm, both generals being killed.

Monuments are erected to both commanders. There is also an obelisk to their memory in the Government gardens, near the Fort, overlooking the river.

Another drive is through Beauport—a village entirely French—to the Falls of Montmorency, situate in a park of fine forest trees. The torrent falls into a pool of immense depth, and passes through a natural tunnel of rock to the river—that is the mass of it, some running away across the flat tables of rock. This was the scene of a terrible catastrophe. There are now standing on either side of this magnificent waterfall two piers, the remains of a suspension bridge erected by the owner of the park. When completed, a waggon, containing two or three people, including a lady, essayed to cross, but on reaching the centre the suspending rods gave way and the whole bridge fell, precipitating the unfortunate people into the torrent; not a trace of either passengers, horse, or waggon, ever being discovered.

Lorette, an Indian village ten miles distant,

affords an interesting excursion — the route yielding fine views of the St. Charles's River. This village is inhabited by North American Indians, comprising a population of four hundred. They manufacture snow shoes, mocassins, and other curiosities. In winter the men go twenty or thirty miles away into the mountains to hunt the moose, cariboo (a small species of moose), bears, and small fur-bearing animals, with which this region abounds.

We pay a visit to the Grand Chief Paul, who is very affable, and pleased to exhibit the various medals presented to his ancestors by King George, for their services on our behalf against the French, and one presented to himself by her Majesty; also his tomahawk and calumet (the pipe of peace), with many articles of his tribe's manufacture, some of which we purchase.

Bidding farewell to the Gibraltar of America, as Quebec may be styled, we journey back to Montreal by the great steamer "Quebec" up the St. Lawrence—a most enjoyable evening on the water—meeting several rafts of timber on our way up, also many fine vessels.

The cliffs and banks on either side vary much in appearance, being in some places steep and densely wooded, in others low, with gently sloping meadows. The little white houses along the bank appear almost continuous, and the small villages numberless.

As night advances, we are entertained on the main deck with a capital string band, the purser and one of the stewards at intervals dancing Scotch reels, Irish jigs and breakdowns in an accomplished style, that fairly brings down the ship.

A run up the St. Lawrence in one of these vessels, lofty between decks, with large well-ventilated state rooms, and a well-managed cuisine, will satisfy the most fastidious. They are great favourites, and universally patronised by all travelling between Montreal and Quebec. Leaving Quebec at four P.M., we spend an amusing evening, enjoy as good a night's rest as if in an hotel, and rise in the morning at half-past five to go ashore at Montreal, where we arrived at half-past four A.M., having accomplished the distance of one hundred-and-eighty miles in twelve-and-a-half hours,—upwards of fourteen miles an hour.

CHAPTER XXI.

LAKES CHAMPLAIN AND GEORGE.

LAST OF CANADA—LAKE CHAMPLAIN—ADIRONDACK AND GREEN MOUNTAINS—LAKE GEORGE—THE ISLANDS—A SALUTE—FORT WILLIAM HENRY HOTEL—A DRIVE TO GLENN'S FALLS.

REMAINING another day at Montreal, to give a last fond look, like the tearful soldier, we leave by six o'clock train the following morning for Rouse's Point, fifty miles distant, and stepping on board the steamer "Vermont," here bid farewell to Canada, and are once more in the States. The run from this, the extreme north of Lake Champlain, down to Fort Ticonderoga, gives us more than a hundred miles of fine bold scenery. We pass many little hamlets, situated on the shores of the Lake, Burlington, a large manufacturing town, and also notice many curious rocks and islands, the abode of numerous gulls and water fowl. The two ranges of mountains, the Green Mountains of Vermont on our right, and Adirondacks on our left, are the chief objects of interest. Arriving at Fort Ticonderoga, a ruin, we have a short run in open cars to Baldwin, at the end of Lake George, where we again take steamer, the "Minne-ha-ha" (Indian for laughing water) down the Lake. This is the most beautiful lake we have seen for striking scenery. We call at several small places on the banks, passing through the countless islands with which the transparent waters of the lake are thickly studded. Many of these little lands have a house and boathouse erected upon them, the summer retreats of some of the business men of New York.

Only thirty-five miles in length, it appears small after the inland seas that bear the title of lake, but the proximity of the bold headlands and high peaks jutting out of this wild and picturesque sheet of water render it unique in its exquisite beauty. As we approach the end of the Lake, and near the pier opposite the Fort William Henry Hotel, a gun is fired as a salute, its echoes reverberating down the land-locked lake, and on running alongside a band on the lawn strikes up a welcome. This reception of the steamer is the event of the day, and the guests here turn out to meet the new arrivals.

The Fort William Henry Hotel is a handsome and extensive building, on rising ground, and looking straight down the Lake, commanding a magnificent prospect. It is a fashionable resort, and we find some hundreds of guests assembled. The grounds attached to the hotel are extensive and shady, and the mornings are spent in rambling along the shore, and boating, or playing at croquet, archery, or bowls. There is also some capital fishing a few miles down among some of the little islands. The Lake teems with fish, and from the pier may be seen hundreds of fine perch.

A band performs during the day, and if wet, under the long-roofed terrace, running the whole length of the hotel, while every evening there is dancing in the capacious drawing room.

There is also a fine billiard saloon, and everything that can be desired in the way of a first-rate hotel. The scenery round is wooded, and some delightful drives may be had.

On the other side of the village, after clambering and scrambling over rocks and through bushes, we find a suitable place for a dip, and indulge in a glorious swim in these clear deep waters.

Our next halt is to be at Saratoga Springs, reached from here by stage coach for nine miles, a beautiful drive over a planked road, passing Bloody Pond, once filled with dead soldiers, flung into its water in lieu of burial. We next reach Glenn's Falls, a smart little town on the Hudson, with many pretty residences, whence we take the rail by a branch line, changing at Fort Edward into the cars of the Saratoga and Washington Railroad, to Saratoga Springs.

CHAPTER XXII.

SARATOGA.

MONSTER HOTELS—THE GRAND UNION—SOCIETY—
LIFE IN THE STREETS—THE SPRINGS—THE RACE
COURSE—LAKE SARATOGA—GLEN MITCHELL—
A GARDEN PARTY—YOUTHFUL AMERICA—
DRESS AND DIAMONDS.

THIS celebrated spa has often been termed the American Brighton, but it unquestionably is unique in its appearance, habits, and general character.

The most striking feature first noticed by the new comer is the group of monster hotels in the centre of the village, and which are unequalled in any other city in the States.

Congress Hall, the Grand Union, and the United States hotels are all close together, the first two standing opposite each other on either side of the

Broadway, the principal and central street. The streets are well planted with trees, and as life and society are as much out of doors as within, they are much appreciated for their grateful shade. The scene at night, with numerous lamps shining amongst the trees, and the brilliantly-lighted windows of the hotels in the background, is very gay and attractive.

The Grand Union, where we stay, is certainly the acmé of grand hotels in this country. It contains one thousand two hundred guests and five hundred servants. There are two miles of halls and corridors, and ten acres of carpet. The drawing-rooms are immense, and the dining-room on a vast scale. A grand ball-room is built in the grounds, in which a ball is held every evening. A beautifully-laid out garden in the rear, with forest trees, forms a square, round which the hotel is built. The rooms overlook these grounds, and balconies run round each floor.

There is a profusion of everything at meals, and fruit and ices in abundance; the victualling department requisitioning quite an army of waiters and attendants, all of whom are black.

This being the very height of the season, we see all the fashion of New York here—senators, judges, governors, members of Congress, and millionaires in plenty. Their families are here for the fixed purpose of doing the grand, and competing in the matter of display. The pleasures of the toilet are freely indulged in, and ladies experience the happiness of appearing in several totally different costumes during the twelve hours.

Though dress is carried to an alarming extent, there is a freedom and ease about the place that will not be repressed. Ladies stroll from one hotel to another, or down the street, without troubling about hats, bonnets, or shawls. The streets resemble a flower show or fashionable pic-nic, while the rows of carriages standing all day opposite these great hotels resemble the outside of the opera on a gala night.

The Springs are, of course, the presumed purport of staying here, and they are wonderful in number and variety. The Congress Spring, in Congress Park, is the first and foremost, the others are distinguished as Columbian, Empire, Excelsior, Hathorn, Seltzer, &c., &c., all differing in their composition and analysis.

The most curious of these natural phenomena are the Geysers, about a mile and a half out of the village. The one known as the Saratoga Geyser, is contained in a building, and being led through a pipe shoots up nearly to the ceiling.

The Champion Spouting Spring is another marvel; this is in the open air, and is brought to the surface from a distance of three hundred feet, this unusual depth having been bored through the solid rock. Its force is restrained by an iron cap over the tube, allowing only a thin stream to come forth. At times this is removed, when a powerful stream spouts upwards to a height of eighty or ninety feet.

The waters of these several springs are put up in bottles and casks, and can be obtained at the chemists' stores in all the principal cities.

These springs are a favourite afternoon rendezvous, and a long stream of carriages may be seen going and returning from three to five.

Another drive is to the race course, small but prettily laid out. It is the property of the Honourable J. Morrissey, Senator and ex-pugilist. The principal summer meeting here attracts thousands, and the excitement and heavy betting over the principal race renders that race the Derby of America.

Lake Saratoga, about four miles out, is another object of interest. It is nine miles long, and between four and five wide. A steam-launch tows a barge from one end to the other, where the white sulphur springs are situate, with an hotel. Picnics and excursions are held here during the summer, the lake also being the scene of the great boat race, in which some ten or twelve Universities are represented.

For lovers of the rod, there are pickerel, black bass, and perch, waiting to be caught in any quantity.

Two miles out along North Broadway, a pleasant and shady road brings us to Glen Mitchell, a great running and trotting ground, the periodical agricultural shows being also held here; and at the hotel adjoining are some picturesque woods in the rear, most agreeable for a ramble and retreat from the sun.

It will thus be seen that there is no lack of walks and drives (the latter always freely watered) for those that way inclined; while the evenings are of course spent at the hotels, which, besides their own dances, occasionally give a grand ball, to which the guests at the other hotels are invited.

Whilst here, the Grand Union inaugurate a new species of entertainment, by issuing invites to a grand garden party, to which as guests we receive an invitation. The balconies around are draped with divers colours, and an immense American banner, with many smaller cnes, decorate the trees. Swings have been erected for the children, and a platform for their dancing. At four P.M. the band strikes up, the company now fast assembling. They are quite a study, and we have the pleasure of seeing all the pick of American society.

The children are dressed superbly, the smallest dots of all being little clouds of lace. Young ladies, of the more advanced age of seven and upwards, are costumed like little women, with high boots, silk stockings, and jewellery, all wearing necklaces, earrings, bracelets, and rings.

Two little eight-year old blondes waltz together in such beautiful style, that they are the admired of all admirers, and appear like fairies in flesh and blood.

When the platform is filled, with some eighty children dancing, the effect is really charming, and they all have a self-possession that nothing seems to ruffle. The absence of anything like shyness is noticeable with all.

Two children of about eleven, a girl and boy, particularly attract our attention; the former in deep blue—hat, silk dress, silk stockings, boots, fan, &c., all *en suite;* the latter, a handsome fair boy, is in appearance, a little courtier, come out of one of Sir Peter Lely's pictures—jacket to the waist, with belt and breeches to the knee of deep blue velvet, blue silk stockings, shoes with buckles, and deep lace collar, back and front, with cuffs of same materials.

The girls are all exquisitely got up, regardless of cost, and dressed like princesses, with gold vinaigrettes and fans by their side, and kid gloves with six or eight buttons even at the age of five. Their nurses are in attendance, and all uniformly dressed, with mob caps.

The dresses of the ladies are most extravagant, but as a rule in excellent taste. In an assemblage of some two or three thousand, there are of course some exceptions, and a few have overdone it altogether. The display of diamonds is something extraordinary; they are the rage with New York society, and some of the millionaires' wives are carrying thousands and thousands upon their persons. For the first time in our travels, we note here many excessively stout ladies, some ludicrously so. The girls are elegant, but I can see many who promise in a few years to pull down the scales with their mammas. Their great anxiety seems to be how to sit down gracefully, rather a difficult matter under existing fashions, and incurring a kind of side movement, followed on rising by a general spasmodic pulling out of puffs belonging to the panier or whatever the excrescence in the rear is now styled.

The papers here comment upon the great lack of "marrying young men" coming forward with offers, but excuses them for the natural fear they experience as to the necessary funds being forthcoming.

Certainly, to see some of the girls, with hundreds of dollars trailing in the dust, it would shake the nerves of any man unless he have expectations from Uncle Crœsus.

Taken altogether, the variety of costumes have a charming effect of colour, and many twine a white gauze cloud round their heads, with the ends streaming, after the manner of brides.

The appearance of our own sex needs no description; they are simply the antipodes of all that is bright and gay, being dressed in decent mourning, and serve as a foil to the gay colours before mentioned.

Before quitting the subject of dress, I must notice the beautiful boots worn by the women throughout the States. Feet are always smart, with poor as well as rich.

CHAPTER XXIII.

THE MIGHTY HUDSON.

ALBANY AND ITS TRADE—HUDSON RIVER STEAMERS—
THE CATSKILL MOUNTAINS—RIP VAN WINKLE—
FISHKILL MOUNTAINS — RIVER SCENERY —
WEST POINT—SING SING—THE PALISADES
—NEW YORK BAY.

ONE hour and a half's rail from Saratoga brings us to the City of Albany, capital of the State of New York, situated on the west bank of the Hudson River, a great railway bridge connecting it with East Albany on the opposite side. In the centre is a swinging bridge, to allow the multitude of lumber and timber vessels to pass through.

Albany is an old city, attractive in appearance, with wide streets, fine churches, and public buildings.

The capitol stands on an eminence, surrounded by trees, and a new State building is in course of erection on a colossal scale. The City Hall and Exchange also are both fine public edifices.

The trade here is great, and foundries and breweries are to be seen on a great scale. One brewery sends out seventy thousand barrels annually. Lumber and cattle are two other important branches of commerce the communications by rail and water affording every facility.

Leaving the Delavan House on a brilliant summer' morning, we embark on board the steamer "C. Vibbard" for a run down this famous river to New York.

These steamers are again an example of the perfection to which river travelling may be brought With an enormous beam, they yet possess fine lines fore and aft at the water-line, and although resembling huge floating hotels in appearance, and appearing almost cumbersome, yet maintain a speed throughout of fifteen miles an hour, including stoppages. They are driven by immense paddle-wheels and great horse power.

Passing many minor places on the banks, the first point of interest is the City of Hudson, one hundred and fifteen miles from New York, beautifully situated on a promontory, running out into the river. Exactly opposite is the village of Athens, and four miles beyond we reach Catskill and the Catskill Mountains

HUDSON RIVER.

with the Mountain House Hotel, three thousand feet above the river and eight miles distant, appearing like a patch of snow on the mountain. It is a favourite summer resort, and the air of the mountains clear and bracing. Nestled among these mountains is the little white cabin where Rip Van Winkle laid down to take his protracted slumber—at least so runs the legend. These mountains vary much in their different aspects, and contain several waterfalls. German Town, Barry Town, with Cruger's Island, Kingston, and other places are passed, the banks acquiring a most precipitous character as we pass Hyde Park and Poughkeepsie, five miles lower down, a town of considerable size, whose steeples may be seen from some distance.

The Chawangung and Fishkill Mountains next rise into view; every bend of the river offering a new scene, and presenting a magnificent living panorama. At one time we can fancy ourselves on an Italian lake, apparently shut in by huge mountains; then, turning sharply round, almost at right angles, an unbroken sheet of water for miles meets our view, the scenes changing as continually and completely as the glass in a kaleidoscope.

West Point, the seat of the great Military Academy, is one of the principal places of interest on the river. Little of this can be seen from the water. The scenery, however, is remarkably picturesque, and Cozzen's Hotel can be seen standing prominently out against the sky.

Twenty miles further we pass Sing Sing, with its great white low-lying convict prison. Irvington, named after Washington Irving, whose house may be sighted from the steamer; Piermont, Yonkers, and Riverdale are passed, and we reach Fort Lee, the commencement of that natural wonder the Palisades. Three to five hundred feet in height, these perpendicular and unbroken walls of rock, resembling columns, like the Giants' Causeway, stretch for twenty miles, their summits fringed with pine trees, and appearing grand and gloomy. The opposite side is studded with splendid buildings and handsome residences, with beautiful grounds sloping to the river. The water is clear, and not a weed to be seen anywhere, even in the creeks.

With Fort Washington astern, we are now rapidly approaching the suburbs of New York, and have a fine view of New Jersey City and Hoboken; and, as we enter the crowded waters, alive with every description of craft, New York Bay, the Narrows, and Staten Islands come into view in the opposite direction.

So delightful is this journey down the most magnificent piece of river scenery in the world, that it is with deep regret we leave the vessel for New York

City. For calm, tranquil enjoyment, with a world of beauty upon which to feast the eye, it cannot be surpassed. The laziest of travellers and lotus-eaters can, by a summer trip on the Hudson River, have scenes of beauty brought before him that would repay a hundred-fold the greatest exertions of the most untiring scene-hunter.

CHAPTER XXIV.

HOMEWARD BOUND.

MONEY CHANGING — FAREWELL — SANDY HOOK — SALOON LIST—GLOBE TROTTERS—PORPOISES— OCEAN SPRAY—SIGNALLING—IRELAND— OUR COUSINS—LIVERPOOL— HOME AGAIN.

ONCE more in New York City, we have only a day to spare before sailing. We transmute the rolls of dirty, but official, paper we possess into that superior hardware, British gold, and wander about Fifth Avenue and Broadway until a silent monitor admonishes us that it is time to take our farewell American dinner at the St. Nicholas.

The morning of our departure resembles the one of arrival in this city, a pouring rain making everything and everybody appear miserable. We sail at noon, and have to cross to New Jersey, where the Cunard Docks are situate. Our ship is lying alongside, and we go on board in a tremendous rain.

Almost imperceptibly we move slowly from the quay, and can distinguish our Virginian fellow-traveller and another friend waving their handkerchiefs and umbrellas, amongst a crowd of some two hundred people at the end of the Dock Pier, until the big ship has glided out into space, and with her now quickly throbbing screw is fast leaving Jersey City and New York behind in the mist and rain.

In about two hours we drop our pilot off Sandy Hook, and with that lightship see the last of Yankeedom.

The southerly wind has not kicked up the sea outside that every one expected, and the weather for the first three days is close and oppressive, with a smooth sea.

We have a large passenger list, this being a favourite vessel, and having her state rooms booked for her three following voyages. We number one hundred and twenty-eight in the saloon, amongst whom are many Americans, some senators, judges, &c., also one old gentleman completing the tour round the world.

The best time of year for this tour is to start in October, so doing India, China, and Japan in the winter months. Tickets for the round tour can be obtained extending over twelve months, and the "Globe trotters," as they are termed, can lie over when and where they please.

We have some celebrated actors amongst our list, and a mixed entertainment of singing, recitations, &c., is given one evening, several amateurs assisting. The hat is passed round after the performance, and the proceeds given to the Seamen's Widows and Orphans' Society.

We pass one morning through a school of about two hundred porpoises, leaping four and five feet out of the water, and appearing to be extremely delighted about some private affairs of their own, travelling through the water at a great speed.

Not until we near mid-ocean do we feel the real movement of the Atlantic, when with a strong head wind and a heavy swell running across our bows, the mighty vessel plunges her great snout into the blue hills of water, throwing the heavy spray over her forecastle to the foremast, and as the lifting of her stern brings the screw above the surface, trembles and shivers again with the increased vibration. It is quite a treat after the hot weather, and the air imparts a delicious feeling, although it causes some to appear pensive or reflective who have been amongst the loudest in still water.

We meet several vessels, and the signalling on a dark night by coloured lights and rockets is very pretty, as we go plunging on in the darkness with a regular swing and roll, except now and then when a rather taller swell than usual gives us an extra lift.

The passage much resembles the one out, and with pleasant company on board, an extensive library, fine air, a good cigar, and perfect health, we do not find the time hang heavily on our hands, but enjoy ourselves to the full.

The sea is a dead calm as we sight the Irish coast off the Fastnet, where we signal the Telegraph Station and passing three hours after the Old Head of Kinsale, with its great striped Lighthouse, are soon lying off Queenstown.

A glorious summer day is now on, and the tender comes alongside with several ladies, taking off a few of our passengers and the numerous mail bags, we having brought the heavy mails for Europe.

A White Star and an Inman steamer are just starting westward, while we, casting off the tender, speed on for the Mersey.

This being the last evening, we have a merry gathering in the smoking-room on deck, with songs of all kinds, our cousins heartily joining in "Rule Britannia," while we respond to the "Star Spangled Banner." We come on deck in the morning to find a strong breeze blowing; the waves white with foam, and the Welsh mountains forming a grey background to a large ship being towed up channel, while on our port side, is a fine three-masted schooner, lying down to it, and scratching along to the westward.

Reaching the mouth of the Mersey, we amuse ourselves by fooling round the light ship for an hour, until the depth of water allows us to cross the bar, when we are soon at our moorings off the dock entrance, and are transferred to the pigmy "Satellite," which deposits us on the quay.

A few hours more and we are again in "famous London Town," having covered by sea and land upwards of fifteen thousand miles.

Thus we bring the sketch of a most enjoyable and satisfactory tour to a conclusion. If it tempt others to do likewise, they will, we are satisfied, be gratified fully as much as ourselves. The grandest and most superb river scenery in the world, the most majestic waterfalls, immense lakes, gigantic mountains, and exquisite landscapes offer to the lover of the picturesque a series of natural wonders elsewhere unrivalled; while giant cities, noble buildings, palatial hotels, and unequalled excellence in steamship and railway transit, altogether present a combination of attractions to be met with nowhere but "Under the Gridiron."

CHAPTER XXV.

THE AMERICAN PEOPLE.

ENERGY—LEVELLING—REPRESENTATION—BRAG—
STOREKEEPERS—GENERAL CHARACTER.

A FEW remarks as to my general impressions of the American people themselves may not be inappropriate before concluding.

One cannot be long amongst them without feeling, by their manners and deportment, that they are, as a people, thoroughly satisfied with their position as a nation, which they consider to be at the very top of the tree.

Their universally-acknowledged character is that of " Go ahead," which truly describes their nature. The rapid strides they take in commerce, and the energy displayed in extending their cities is wonderful. They keep close to trade, grudging the hours spent on recreation. The real, thorough-going Yankee, however, carries this pushing manner with him, even outside the pale of business, frequently to the detriment of that interchange of courtesies so justly appreciated.

He is no respecter of persons or things. To level all classes of society is his chief aim and boast, and the cab-driver or railway porter shakes hands, and is "Hail fellow well met" with those who in this country would be far above him in the social scale. The advantages derived from this "rough and tumble" kind of equality are somewhat questionable, as it is apt to beget a familiarity that may, when carried to an extreme, become offensive.

We may, I think, attribute this, without fear of contradiction, to the system of their Government and status of their representatives. No one knows who may suddenly rise to office and power, or, on the other hand, who may fall as quickly. The small storekeeper of to-day may be the holder of an influential office in the space of a few months, hence the openly-avowed equality, perhaps not secretly acknowledged.

Too often the man of low degree and needy circumstances is brought prominently forward, and mainly on account of these qualifications swept by the mass into office. To such an extent is this now carried, that poverty is exalted and wealth is in reality a drawback and impediment to the ambitious public individual.

As the result of making a lack of means a claim to

the people's support, is it to be wondered at that too often the emoluments of office render the office-holder unscrupulous, and willing to become the slave of his party and constituents so long as he can retain the position he has achieved? This is becoming a serious matter, and one that occupies the thoughts of all reflective and deep-thinking Americans having the interests of their country really at heart, who do not fail to perceive and deplore that it has reached a dangerous extreme.

We are constantly reminded that America is a great country, and a young one, and that they have driven her along at a great pace. A great country she most unquestionably is; in fact, for many purposes, considerably too great, if we may judge by the conflicting and rival interests of the several States (some separated by thousands of miles) which constantly bring matters in their House of Congress to a dead-lock. There is also such a state of affairs as being over-driven. Bancroft

In speaking of the Americans as a people, there are a large class—intellectual, scientific, and refined—whom I do not for a moment include in these remarks. They, however, keep retired, and will not, or do not, come forward to take any part in public life. Hence, as a traveller, I speak of the American as I find him at the hotels, on the steamer and railway, or out West.

Notorious for "brag" as he is, I was prepared to

believe that trait in his character had been exaggerated and over-drawn, but am forced to admit there is much truth in the accusation. No matter what part of the country one is in, or what specimen of nature or art may be in question—wherever may be the locality to which he belongs, there is to be found "the finest in the world." This is a stock phrase, and a part of his creed he is never tired of quoting. Some, again, speak of their country and its great natural beauties as if due to their own individual foresight and exertion, and I doubt not feel complacently satisfied at the compliment they pay the Almighty by flying the American flag over the wonders of His creation.

There is also, in the stores, a very marked want of that inviting civility so attractive to the customer. Wares are not brought forward from which he may select. He is asked which it is he wants, and is told the price, when he can take it or leave it, as he thinks fit, without comment. As a London citizen, this impolicy in business really surprises me, and I can only attribute it to the independent spirit that considers civility as a toll upon liberty.

It is in the interest of intending tourists that I make mention of this, that they may not consider this abruptness as anything out of the common. It is not intended for discourtesy, but only as an assertion of equality.

Honest in purpose, hard-working, of great determination, kind-hearted, fearless, and with a rich vein of humour underlying their nature, the people of this great republic are, as a body, greatly to be admired and respected. With a natural leaning towards the new, they yet cherish a love for the old, to which the multitude of American visitors that sweep over Europe each succeeding summer amply testify. Whether in Switzerland, Italy, or the East, their names in the hotel-books far outnumber those of other nationalities, while Great Britain and Ireland receive a large share of visitors to what they still call "The Old Country."

Their feelings towards us are unquestionably those of friendship, and, speaking the same tongue, with our interests so much in common, there should be amongst nations no firmer friends than England and the United States of America.

TABLE OF RAILWAY DISTANCES

And time occupied in direct journeys between New York and the following principal cities and places :—

Note.—This Table I have compiled with great care from several time tables and maps, and believe the figures to be substantially correct.

Place.	Length of Journey.	Distance.
Albany, N. Y. ...	... 5 hours	... 143 miles
,, by Hudson River boat	9 ,,	... 144 ,,
Austin, Texas ...	... 4 days	... 1876 ,,
Baltimore, Md. ...	... 7 hours	... 188 ,,
Boston, Mass. ...	... 7 ,,	... 236 ,,
,, by Fall River route	... 14¼ ,,	... 269 ,,
Buffalo, N. Y. ...	... 16½ ,,	... 439 ,,
Burlington, Iowa	... 43 ,,	... 1077 ,,
Cairo, Ill. ...	... 47½ ,,	... 1099 ,,
Charleston, S. C.	... 40 ,,	... 911 ,,
Chicago, Ill. ...	... 37 ,,	... 913 ,,
Cincinnati, O. ...	... 29½ ,,	... 757 ,,
Cleveland, O. ...	... 23 ,,	... 622 ,,
Columbus, O ...	... 25 ,,	... 637 ,,
Concord, N. H. ...	... 10 ,,	... 311 ,,
Davenport, Iowa.	... 46 ,,	... 1096 ,,
Denver, Col. ...	... 3 days 18 hours	... 2012 ,,
Detroit, Mich. ...	... 26½ hours	... 675 ,,
Erie, Pa. ...	... 19½ ,,	... 527 ,,
Fort Wayne, Ind.	... 29½ ,,	... 764 ,,
Harrisburg, Pa. ...	... 7 ,,	... 195 ,,

RAILWAY DISTANCES, &c.—*Continued.*

Place.	Length of Journey.	Distance.
Hartford, Ct.	4 hours	109 miles
Indianapolis, Ind.	34 ,,	825 ,,
Kansas City, Mo.	2 days 9 hours	1372 ,,
Lake George, N. Y.	9½ hours	212 ,,
Lexington, Va.	26 ,,	554 ,,
Louisville, Ky.	34 ,,	867 ,,
Memphis, Tenn.	2 days 4 hours	1244 ,,
Milwaukee, Wis.	40½ hours	998 ,,
Mobile, Ala.	3 days 5 hours	1600 ,,
Montreal, Can.	17 hours	390 ,,
,, by Lake Champlain route	22 ,,	406 ,,
New Orleans, La.	3 days 7 hours	1647 ,,
Niagara Falls	18 hours	445 ,,
Ogden, Utah	4 days 20 hours	2445 ,,
Omaha, Neb.	2 days 13 hours	1413 ,,
Ottawa, Can.	20 hours	425 ,,
Philadelphia, Pa.	3 ,,	90 ,,
Pittsburgh, Pa.	16½ ,,	444 ,,
Portland, Me.	12 ,,	344 ,,
Poughkeepsie, N. Y.	3 ,,	73 ,,
Providence, R. I.	7½ ,,	185 ,,
Quebec, Can.	23½ ,,	651 ,,
Richmond, Va.	15 ,,	356 ,,
Sacramento, Cal.	6 days 14 hours	3188 ,,
St. Louis, Mo.	43 hours	1064 ,,
St. Paul, Minn.	2 days 14 hours	1322 ,,
Salt Lake City, Utah	5 days	2482 ,,
San Francisco, Cal.	6 days 20 hours	3326 ,,
Saratoga, N. Y.	7 hours	182 ,,

RAILWAY DISTANCES, &c.—*Continued.*

Place.	Length of Journey.	Distance.
Savannah, Ga. ...	46 hours	1018 miles
Syracuse, N. Y....	$12\frac{1}{2}$,,	291 ,,
Toronto, Can. ...	26 ,,	594 ,,
Troy, N. Y. ...	$5\frac{1}{4}$,,	148 ,,
Utica, N. Y. ...	$8\frac{1}{4}$,,	238 ,,
Washington, D. C. ...	$8\frac{1}{2}$,,	230 ,,
White Mountains, N. H.	$15\frac{1}{2}$,,	424 ,,
White Sulphur Springs, Va.	22 ,,	477 ,,
Wilmington, N. C. ...	$27\frac{1}{2}$,,	704 ,,
Yo-Semite Valley, Cal.	8 days 18 hours	3386 ,,

THE FAR WEST.

First Class Fares from New York *via* Omaha.

	Dols.	Cts.
To Omaha	38	00
,, Ogden	115	00
,, Salt Lake City	117	50
,, Sacramento	138	00
,, San Francisco	138	00

An extra charge is made for Drawing-room and Sleeping Cars, to which only first-class passengers are admitted.

	Dols.	Cts.
New York to Omaha	8	00
Omaha to Ogden	8	00
Ogden to San Francisco	6	00
New York to San Francisco	$22	00

These fares are payable in currency, the dollar bill being equal to 3s. 8d., or three dollars to 11s.

FOLKARD & SONS, Printers, 22, Devonshire Street, Queen Square, and 57, Bread Street, Cheapside.

www.ingramcontent.com/pod-product-compliance
Lightning Source LLC
Chambersburg PA
CBHW022116160426
43197CB00009B/1052